Part A: Seasonally Adjusted (by Commodity/Service)

Exhibit 1. U.S. International Trade in Goods and Services

In millions of dollars. Details may not equal totals due to seasonal adjustment and rounding. (R) - Revised.

Period	Balance			Exports			Imports		
	Total	Goods (1)	Services	Total	Goods (1)	Services	Total	Goods (1)	Services
2013									
Jan. - Dec.	-476,392	-701,669	225,276	2,280,194	1,592,784	687,410	2,756,586	2,294,453	462 134
Jan. - Mar.	-120,949	-177,560	56,611	562,411	392,605	169,806	683,360	570,164	113 195
January	-42,205	-61,192	18,987	187,478	130,653	56,825	229,683	191,846	37 838
February	-41,770	-60,688	18,917	188,030	131,420	56,610	229,800	192,107	37 693
March	-36,973	-55,680	18,707	186,903	130,532	56,371	223,876	186,211	37 665
April	-40,417	-58,758	18,342	187,763	131,326	56,437	228,180	190,084	38 096
May	-44,831	-63,352	18,521	187,206	130,319	56,887	232,037	193,671	38 366
June	-36,552	-54,973	18,421	190,366	133,343	57,023	226,918	188,316	38 602
July	-39,419	-58,021	18,603	189,902	132,830	57,072	229,321	190,851	38 470
August	-39,515	-58,527	19,012	190,606	132,829	57,777	230,121	191,356	38 765
September	-42,263	-61,387	19,125	190,249	132,430	57,819	232,512	193,817	38 695
October	-39,083	-57,742	18,659	193,971	136,141	57,829	233,053	193,884	39 170
November	-35,972	-54,765	18,793	194,922	136,752	58,170	230,894	191,517	39 377
December	-37,393	-56,583	19,189	192,799	134,210	58,590	230,193	190,792	39 400
2014									
Jan. - Dec.	-504,711	-735,787	231,076	2,344,528	1,635,133	709,395	2,849,239	2,370,920	478 319
Jan. - Mar.	-123,517	-181,269	57,752	575,003	400,442	174,561	698,520	581,712	116 809
January	-38,841	-59,112	20,271	192,747	133,863	58,884	231,588	192,975	38 613
February	-41,891	-59,955	18,064	188,045	130,669	57,375	229,936	190,624	39 311
March	-42,784	-62,202	19,417	194,212	135,910	58,302	236,997	198,112	38 885
April	-45,583	-65,243	19,660	194,589	135,398	59,192	240,173	200,641	39 532
May	-43,231	-62,751	19,520	196,830	137,235	59,595	240,061	199,986	40 075
June	-41,414	-60,249	18,835	195,970	136,987	58,983	237,383	197,236	40 147
July	-40,655	-59,261	18,606	197,855	139,341	58,514	238,510	198,602	39 908
August	-39,916	-59,485	19,569	198,589	139,296	59,293	238,505	198,781	39 723
September	-43,368	-62,346	18,978	195,185	136,354	58,831	238,553	198,700	39 853
October	-41,898	-61,166	19,268	198,713	138,954	59,759	240,611	200,120	40 491
November	-39,529	-59,000	19,472	196,792	136,909	59,883	236,320	195,909	40 411
December	-45,601	-65,017	19,416	195,002	134,217	60,785	240,603	199,234	41 370
2015									
Jan. - Mar.	-129,936	-188,770	58,834	563,269	381,200	182,070	693,205	569,970	123 236
January	-42,676	-62,533	19,856	189,239	128,539	60,700	231,916	191,072	40 844
February (R)	-35,892	-55,677	19,784	186,193	125,592	60,601	222,085	181,268	40 816
March	-51,367	-70,561	19,193	187,837	127,069	60,769	239,205	197,630	41 575
April									
May									
June									
July									
August									
September									
October									
November									
December									
February data as published last month:	-35,444	-55,176	19,731	186,249	125,637	60,612	221,693	180,813	40 880

(1) Data are presented on a balance of payments (BOP) basis.

NOTE: For information on data sources and methodology, see the information section on page A-1 of this release or at
www.census.gov/ft900 or www.bea.gov/newsreleases/international/trade/tradnewsrelease.htm.

Part A: Seasonally Adjusted (by Commodity/Service)

Exhibit 2. U.S. International Trade in Goods and Services
Three-Month Moving Averages

In millions of dollars. Details may not equal totals due to seasonal adjustment and rounding. (R) - Revised.

Month of Moving Average	Balance			Exports			Imports		
	Total	Goods (1)	Services	Total	Goods (1)	Services	Total	Goods (1)	Services
2013									
January	-42,148	-60,835	18,687	187,843	131,094	56,749	229,991	191,929	38,062
February	-40,537	-59,435	18,898	188,424	131,668	56,756	228,961	191,103	37,857
March	-40,316	-59,187	18,870	187,470	130,868	56,602	227,787	190,055	37,732
April	-39,720	-58,375	18,655	187,565	131,092	56,473	227,285	189,468	37,818
May	-40,740	-59,263	18,523	187,291	130,725	56,565	228,031	189,989	38,042
June	-40,600	-59,028	18,428	188,445	131,663	56,782	229,045	190,690	38,354
July	-40,267	-58,782	18,515	189,158	132,164	56,994	229,425	190,946	38,479
August	-38,495	-57,174	18,679	190,291	133,001	57,290	228,786	190,174	38,612
September	-40,399	-59,312	18,913	190,252	132,696	57,556	230,651	192,008	38,643
October	-40,287	-59,219	18,932	191,608	133,800	57,808	231,895	193,019	38,876
November	-39,106	-57,965	18,859	193,047	135,108	57,940	232,153	193,073	39,080
December	-37,483	-56,363	18,881	193,897	135,701	58,196	231,380	192,064	39,316
2014									
January	-37,402	-56,820	19,418	193,489	134,941	58,548	230,891	191,761	39,130
February	-39,375	-58,550	19,175	191,197	132,914	58,283	230,572	191,464	39,108
March	-41,172	-60,423	19,251	191,668	133,481	58,187	232,840	193,904	38,936
April	-43,420	-62,466	19,047	192,282	133,993	58,290	235,702	196,459	39,243
May	-43,866	-63,398	19,532	195,211	136,181	59,030	239,077	199,580	39,497
June	-43,409	-62,747	19,338	195,796	136,540	59,256	239,206	199,287	39,918
July	-41,766	-60,753	18,987	196,885	137,854	59,031	238,651	198,608	40,044
August	-40,661	-59,665	19,004	197,471	138,541	58,930	238,133	198,206	39,926
September	-41,313	-60,364	19,051	197,210	138,330	58,879	238,522	198,694	39,828
October	-41,727	-60,999	19,272	197,496	138,201	59,294	239,223	199,200	40,023
November	-41,598	-60,838	19,239	196,896	137,406	59,491	238,495	198,243	40,252
December	-42,343	-61,728	19,385	196,836	136,693	60,142	239,178	198,421	40,757
2015									
January	-42,602	-62,183	19,581	193,678	133,222	60,456	236,280	195,405	40,875
February (R)	-41,390	-61,075	19,685	190,145	129,449	60,695	231,535	190,525	41,010
March	-43,312	-62,923	19,611	187,756	127,067	60,690	231,068	189,990	41,079
April									
May									
June									
July									
August									
September									
October									
November									
December									

(1) Data are presented on a BOP basis.

NOTES:

* The three-month moving averages shown in this exhibit are computed by summing the subject month and the two prior months, dividing by three, and showing the average at the end month of the period. A moving average is useful in smoothing the volatile trade data so that trends can better be discerned.

* For information on data sources and methodology, see the information section on page A-1 of this release or at www.census.gov/ft900 or www.bea.gov/newsreleases/international/trade/tradnewsrelease.htm.

Part A: Seasonally Adjusted (by Commodity/Service)

Exhibit 3. U.S. Exports of Services by Major Category

In millions of dollars. Details may not equal totals due to seasonal adjustment and rounding. (R) - Revised.

Period	Total Services	Maintenance and Repair Services n.i.e.	Transport	Travel (for all purposes including education) (1)	Insurance Services	Financial Services	Charges for the Use of Intellectual Property n.i.e.	Telecommuni-cations, Computer, and Information Services	Other Business Services	Government Goods and Services n.i.e.
2013										
Jan. - Dec.	687,410	16,295	87,267	173,131	16,096	84,066	129,178	33,409	123,447	24,522
Jan. - Mar.	169,806	3,441	21,873	42,700	4,010	20,393	32,248	8,283	30,555	6,303
January	56,825	1,196	7,250	14,232	1,357	6,828	10,775	2,773	10,296	2,117
February	56,610	1,131	7,350	14,254	1,333	6,792	10,735	2,752	10,165	2,099
March	56,371	1,114	7,273	14,214	1,320	6,773	10,738	2,758	10,094	2,087
April	56,437	1,126	7,253	14,093	1,316	6,912	10,786	2,793	10,084	2,073
May	56,887	1,162	7,324	14,249	1,318	7,011	10,829	2,814	10,106	2,073
June	57,023	1,239	7,302	14,294	1,326	6,936	10,868	2,820	10,161	2,077
July	57,072	1,439	7,026	14,368	1,339	6,862	10,903	2,811	10,248	2,076
August	57,777	1,528	7,116	14,801	1,349	6,870	10,880	2,800	10,326	2,107
September	57,819	1,557	7,193	14,572	1,356	7,002	10,798	2,786	10,395	2,160
October	57,829	1,618	7,235	14,562	1,359	7,329	10,658	2,770	10,456	1,842
November	58,170	1,616	7,365	14,671	1,361	7,383	10,596	2,764	10,522	1,892
December	58,590	1,568	7,580	14,820	1,360	7,369	10,612	2,769	10,593	1,919
2014										
Jan. - Dec.	709,395	18,710	90,237	176,951	16,728	88,418	132,653	33,356	128,527	23,815
Jan. - Mar.	174,561	4,223	22,028	44,055	4,007	21,180	32,758	8,057	31,687	6,565
January	58,884	1,449	7,510	15,205	1,343	7,169	10,816	2,707	10,570	2,115
February	57,375	1,370	7,094	14,185	1,333	6,984	10,938	2,676	10,561	2,233
March	58,302	1,404	7,424	14,665	1,332	7,026	11,005	2,675	10,556	2,216
April	59,192	1,459	7,428	14,879	1,366	7,499	11,190	2,774	10,413	2,182
May	59,595	1,517	7,626	15,113	1,387	7,604	11,274	2,829	10,341	1,904
June	58,983	1,530	7,382	14,801	1,393	7,602	11,309	2,841	10,340	1,784
July	58,514	1,586	7,450	14,419	1,409	7,209	11,029	2,817	10,753	1,842
August	59,293	1,661	7,719	14,859	1,421	7,027	10,931	2,804	10,992	1,879
September	58,831	1,630	7,551	14,411	1,429	7,149	10,930	2,801	11,029	1,901
October	59,759	1,679	7,619	14,693	1,434	7,600	11,027	2,808	10,993	1,907
November	59,883	1,697	7,545	14,840	1,439	7,570	11,089	2,812	10,974	1,918
December	60,785	1,728	7,888	14,881	1,444	7,978	11,115	2,812	11,007	1,933
2015										
Jan. - Mar.	182,070	5,137	22,733	45,070	4,378	23,592	33,374	8,442	33,451	5,893
January	60,700	1,666	7,631	15,097	1,451	7,887	11,117	2,809	11,092	1,952
February (R)	60,601	1,715	7,488	15,040	1,459	7,838	11,125	2,812	11,157	1,966
March	60,769	1,756	7,614	14,932	1,469	7,867	11,132	2,822	11,202	1,975
April										
May										
June										
July										
August										
September										
October										
November										
December										
February data as published last month:										
	60,612	1,715	7,470	15,158	1,459	7,750	11,125	2,812	11,157	1,966

n.i.e. Not included elsewhere

(1) All travel purposes include 1) business travel, including expenditures by border, seasonal, and other short-term workers and 2) personal travel, including health-related and education-related travel.

NOTE: For information on data sources, methodology, and definitions, see the information section on page A-1 of this release or at www.census.gov/ft900 or www.bea.gov/newsreleases/international/trade/tradnewsrelease.htm.

Part A: Seasonally Adjusted (by Commodity/Service)

Exhibit 4. U.S. Imports of Services by Major Category

In millions of dollars. Details may not equal totals due to seasonal adjustment and rounding. (R) - Revised.

Period	Total Services	Maintenance and Repair Services n.i.e.	Transport	Travel (for all purposes including education) (1)	Insurance Services	Financial Services	Charges for the Use of Intellectual Property n.i.e.	Telecommuni- cations, Computer, and Information Services	Other Business Services	Government Goods and Services n.i.e.
2013										
Jan. - Dec.	462,134	7,620	90,754	104,677	50,454	18,683	39,015	32,877	92,710	25,343
Jan. - Mar.	113,195	1,870	22,457	25,664	12,507	4,378	10,003	7,845	22,107	6,364
January	37,838	627	7,459	8,510	4,223	1,479	3,406	2,597	7,397	2,139
February	37,693	614	7,602	8,518	4,149	1,433	3,321	2,601	7,340	2,115
March	37,665	628	7,396	8,636	4,135	1,466	3,275	2,647	7,370	2,111
April	38,096	644	7,453	8,676	4,180	1,523	3,270	2,737	7,487	2,126
May	38,366	659	7,497	8,658	4,226	1,560	3,246	2,787	7,598	2,134
June	38,602	657	7,527	8,768	4,274	1,537	3,204	2,798	7,702	2,135
July	38,470	667	7,459	8,657	4,323	1,524	3,143	2,769	7,799	2,129
August	38,765	668	7,543	8,827	4,323	1,513	3,130	2,759	7,882	2,120
September	38,695	658	7,519	8,662	4,274	1,588	3,165	2,767	7,953	2,108
October	39,170	603	7,685	8,886	4,176	1,674	3,249	2,793	8,010	2,094
November	39,377	596	7,866	8,862	4,106	1,702	3,297	2,808	8,062	2,077
December	39,400	598	7,748	9,018	4,066	1,682	3,308	2,814	8,110	2,056
2014										
Jan. - Dec.	478,319	7,590	94,410	111,714	49,315	19,658	41,940	33,261	96,609	23,822
Jan. - Mar.	116,809	1,820	22,960	26,439	11,966	4,623	10,514	8,276	24,155	6,057
January	38,613	598	7,573	8,722	4,021	1,593	3,255	2,772	8,044	2,036
February	39,311	606	7,597	8,798	3,986	1,500	4,012	2,753	8,045	2,014
March	38,885	616	7,791	8,919	3,959	1,529	3,247	2,751	8,066	2,007
April	39,532	656	7,772	9,252	4,078	1,586	3,340	2,756	8,050	2,043
May	40,075	664	7,866	9,523	4,132	1,624	3,386	2,765	8,065	2,051
June	40,147	677	7,741	9,499	4,122	1,647	3,535	2,778	8,112	2,037
July	39,908	649	7,794	9,376	4,105	1,655	3,576	2,777	7,999	1,978
August	39,723	619	7,847	9,302	4,111	1,658	3,514	2,777	7,953	1,942
September	39,853	614	7,940	9,250	4,141	1,712	3,521	2,778	7,972	1,926
October	40,491	619	8,011	9,654	4,207	1,729	3,504	2,780	8,056	1,931
November	40,411	629	7,987	9,539	4,221	1,697	3,511	2,785	8,111	1,931
December	41,370	642	8,492	9,881	4,232	1,727	3,540	2,791	8,136	1,927
2015										
Jan. - Mar.	123,236	1,848	24,839	29,292	12,524	5,290	10,885	8,416	24,411	5,732
January	40,844	620	8,113	9,715	4,188	1,754	3,593	2,799	8,143	1,918
February (R)	40,816	608	8,078	9,714	4,169	1,764	3,632	2,806	8,135	1,910
March	41,575	620	8,648	9,863	4,167	1,772	3,660	2,811	8,133	1,903
April										
May										
June										
July										
August										
September										
October										
November										
December										
February data as published last month:										
	40,880	608	8,051	9,800	4,169	1,769	3,632	2,806	8,135	1,910

n.i.e. Not included elsewhere

(1) All travel purposes include 1) business travel, including expenditures by border, seasonal, and other short-term workers and 2) personal travel, including health-related and education-related travel.

NOTE: For information on data sources, methodology, and definitions, see the information section on page A-1 of this release or at www.census.gov/ft900 or www.bea.gov/newsreleases/international/trade/tradnewsrelease.htm.

Part A: Seasonally Adjusted (by Commodity/Service)

Exhibit 5. U.S. Trade in Goods

In millions of dollars. Details may not equal totals due to seasonal adjustment and rounding. (R) - Revised.

Period	Balance		Exports			Imports		
	Total Balance of Payments Basis	Total Census Basis	Total Balance of Payments Basis	Net Adjustments	Total Census Basis	Total Balance of Payments Basis	Net Adjustments	Total Census Basis
2013								
Jan. - Dec.	-701,669	-688,728	1,592,784	13,191	1,579,593	2,294,453	26,131	2,268,321
Jan. - Mar.	-177,560	-174,600	392,605	3,619	388,986	570,164	6,578	563,586
January	-61,192	-60,576	130,653	1,494	129,159	191,846	2,111	189,735
February	-60,688	-59,282	131,420	932	130,488	192,107	2,338	189,769
March	-55,680	-54,742	130,532	1,193	129,339	186,211	2,130	184,081
April	-58,758	-57,638	131,326	1,003	130,323	190,084	2,123	187,962
May	-63,352	-62,293	130,319	963	129,356	193,671	2,022	191,648
June	-54,973	-53,568	133,343	632	132,711	188,316	2,037	186,279
July	-58,021	-57,021	132,830	1,173	131,657	190,851	2,174	188,377
August	-58,527	-57,606	132,829	1,305	131,524	191,356	2,227	189,129
September	-61,387	-60,416	132,430	1,147	131,282	193,817	2,118	191,699
October	-57,742	-56,483	136,141	926	135,215	193,884	2,185	191,698
November	-54,765	-53,845	136,752	1,354	135,398	191,517	2,274	189,243
December	-56,583	-55,258	134,210	1,068	133,141	190,792	2,393	188,399
2014								
Jan. - Dec.	-735,787	-721,577	1,635,133	11,936	1,623,197	2,370,920	26,146	2,344,774
Jan. - Mar.	-181,269	-177,092	400,442	2,962	397,480	581,712	7,139	574,573
January	-59,112	-58,442	133,863	1,594	132,269	192,975	2,264	190,711
February	-59,955	-57,750	130,669	190	130,480	190,624	2,395	188,230
March	-62,202	-60,900	135,910	1,179	134,732	198,112	2,480	195,632
April	-65,243	-64,318	135,398	1,205	134,193	200,641	2,130	198,511
May	-62,751	-61,882	137,235	1,267	135,968	199,986	2,135	197,850
June	-60,249	-59,279	136,987	1,155	135,832	197,236	2,126	195,110
July	-59,261	-58,378	139,341	1,271	138,070	198,602	2,155	196,447
August	-59,485	-58,231	139,296	787	138,509	198,781	2,041	196,740
September	-62,346	-60,951	136,354	759	135,595	198,700	2,154	196,546
October	-61,166	-60,046	138,954	950	138,004	200,120	2,070	198,050
November	-59,000	-57,927	136,909	1,049	135,859	195,909	2,123	193,787
December	-65,017	-63,473	134,217	530	133,687	199,234	2,074	197,160
2015								
Jan. - Mar.	-188,770	-185,850	381,200	2,759	378,440	569,970	5,679	564,290
January	-62,533	-61,518	128,539	909	127,630	191,072	1,924	189,148
February (R)	-55,677	-54,570	125,592	812	124,780	181,268	1,919	179,350
March	-70,561	-69,762	127,069	1,038	126,030	197,630	1,837	195,793
April								
May								
June								
July								
August								
September								
October								
November								
December								
February data as published last month:	-55,176	-54,062	125,637	860	124,777	180,813	1,974	178,839

NOTE: For information on data sources, nonsampling errors, definitions, and details concerning what is included in Net Adjustments, see the information section on page A-1 of this release or at www.census.gov/ft900 or www.bea.gov/newsreleases/international/trade/tradnewsrelease.htm.

Part A: Seasonally Adjusted (by Commodity/Service)

Exhibit 6. U.S. Trade in Goods by Principal End-Use Category

In millions of dollars. Details may not equal totals due to seasonal adjustment and rounding. (R) - Revised.

Period	Total Balance of Payments Basis	Net Adjustments	Total Census Basis (1)	End-Use Commodity Category					
				Foods, Feeds, & Beverages	Industrial Supplies (2)	Capital Goods	Automotive Vehicles, etc.	Consumer Goods	Other Goods
Exports									
2014									
Jan. - Dec.	1,635,133	11,936	1,623,197	144,171	506,831	550,046	159,453	199,150	63,545
Jan. - Mar.	400,442	2,962	397,480	36,821	126,142	134,450	37,165	48,494	14,407
January	133,863	1,594	132,269	12,139	43,592	44,491	12,170	15,416	4,462
February	130,669	190	130,480	12,177	40,781	43,845	12,145	16,670	4,862
March	135,910	1,179	134,732	12,505	41,769	46,114	12,851	16,409	5,084
April	135,398	1,205	134,193	12,245	41,967	45,808	12,682	16,333	5,158
May	137,235	1,267	135,968	12,317	42,170	45,644	13,456	16,742	5,638
June	136,987	1,155	135,832	12,045	42,194	45,670	13,620	17,153	5,149
July	139,341	1,271	138,070	11,414	43,483	46,124	15,278	16,505	5,266
August	139,296	787	138,509	10,870	44,220	47,112	13,557	17,268	5,482
September	136,354	759	135,595	12,139	42,151	45,943	13,453	16,582	5,326
October	138,954	950	138,004	12,055	42,069	47,687	13,617	17,019	5,557
November	136,909	1,049	135,859	12,311	42,773	45,377	13,129	16,561	5,710
December	134,217	530	133,687	11,953	39,662	46,231	13,496	16,494	5,851
2015									
Jan. - Mar.	381,200	2,759	378,440	32,629	109,909	135,211	36,318	50,512	13,862
January	128,539	909	127,630	10,894	37,462	45,687	12,546	16,532	4,510
February (R)	125,592	812	124,780	10,701	36,065	44,027	11,490	17,839	4,658
March	127,069	1,038	126,030	11,034	36,382	45,498	12,282	16,141	4,694
April									
May									
June									
July									
August									
September									
October									
November									
December									
Imports									
2014									
Jan. - Dec.	2,370,920	26,146	2,344,774	125,718	665,164	591,001	327,645	557,696	77,550
Jan. - Mar.	581,712	7,139	574,573	29,820	172,618	141,906	77,182	134,654	18,392
January	192,975	2,264	190,711	9,701	57,424	47,668	25,405	44,676	5,836
February	190,624	2,395	188,230	9,538	57,224	46,455	25,529	43,562	5,921
March	198,112	2,480	195,632	10,580	57,971	47,782	26,248	46,416	6,635
April	200,641	2,130	198,511	10,742	57,656	48,616	27,134	47,430	6,933
May	199,986	2,135	197,850	10,588	55,784	49,607	28,508	47,101	6,262
June	197,236	2,126	195,110	10,820	55,404	49,435	27,453	45,654	6,345
July	198,602	2,155	196,447	10,823	55,734	49,078	28,889	45,123	6,801
August	198,781	2,041	196,740	10,530	55,602	50,865	27,496	45,817	6,429
September	198,700	2,154	196,546	10,674	54,556	49,901	26,948	47,730	6,736
October	200,120	2,070	198,050	10,881	54,667	50,882	28,188	46,959	6,474
November	195,909	2,123	193,787	10,399	50,376	50,450	27,513	48,721	6,328
December	199,234	2,074	197,160	10,442	52,767	50,261	28,334	48,507	6,850
2015									
Jan. - Mar.	569,970	5,679	564,290	31,955	132,391	150,644	82,838	145,998	20,465
January	191,072	1,924	189,148	10,627	46,989	50,530	27,801	46,684	6,517
February (R)	181,268	1,919	179,350	10,301	42,784	48,067	26,185	45,151	6,862
March	197,630	1,837	195,793	11,027	42,617	52,047	28,851	54,164	7,086
April									
May									
June									
July									
August									
September									
October									
November									
December									

(1) Detailed data are presented on a Census basis. The information needed to convert to a BOP basis is not available.
(2) Includes petroleum and petroleum products.

NOTE: For information on data sources, nonsampling errors, and definitions, see the information section on page A-1 of this release or at www.census.gov/ft900 or www.bea.gov/newsreleases/international/trade/tradnewsrelease.htm.

Part A: Seasonally Adjusted (by Commodity/Service)

Exhibit 7. U.S. Exports of Goods by End-Use Category and Commodity

In millions of dollars. Details may not equal totals due to seasonal adjustment and rounding. The commodities in this exhibit are ranked on the monthly change within each major commodity grouping. (-) Represents zero or less than one-half of measurement shown. (R) - Revised.

Item (1)	March 2015	February 2015 (R)	Monthly Change	Year-to-Date 2015	Year-to-Date 2014	Year-to-Date Change
Total, Balance of Payments Basis	127,069	125,592	1,477	381,200	400,442	-19,243
Net Adjustments	1,038	812	227	2,759	2,962	-203
Total, Census Basis	126,030	124,780	1,250	378,440	397,480	-19,040
Foods, feeds, and beverages	11,034	10,701	332	32,629	36,821	-4,192
Nuts	1,040	704	337	2,426	2,016	410
Animal feeds, n.e.c.	796	689	108	2,215	2,351	-136
Dairy products and eggs	471	367	104	1,177	1,660	-484
Fish and shellfish	530	466	63	1,453	1,475	-22
Wine, beer, and related products	206	163	43	525	522	3
Sorghum, barley, oats	271	233	38	703	359	344
Oilseeds, food oils	248	217	31	738	788	-50
Fruits, frozen juices	764	734	30	2,217	2,300	-83
Nonagricultural foods, etc.	167	137	29	435	407	29
Other foods	1,105	1,078	27	3,254	3,334	-80
Vegetables	578	575	3	1,729	1,739	-11
Rice	163	161	2	546	539	7
Alcoholic beverages, excluding wine	163	175	-11	502	507	-5
Bakery products	529	545	-15	1,599	1,633	-34
Meat, poultry, etc.	1,516	1,536	-19	4,579	4,882	-303
Wheat	530	575	-45	1,574	2,014	-440
Corn	734	841	-57	2,371	2,720	-349
Soybeans	1,172	1,506	-334	4,588	7,574	-2,987
Industrial supplies and materials	36,382	36,065	317	109,909	126,142	-16,233
Nonmonetary gold	1,971	1,460	511	5,352	7,052	-1,700
Metallurgical grade coal	504	321	183	1,308	1,789	-481
Finished metal shapes	1,727	1,600	127	4,969	5,115	-146
Plastic materials	2,878	2,754	123	8,590	9,243	-653
Agric. industry-unmanufactured	430	326	104	1,043	1,407	-363
Crude oil	593	510	83	1,827	2,149	-322
Gas-natural	488	412	76	1,403	2,150	-747
Agriculture-manufactured, other	283	221	62	739	726	12
Other industrial supplies	2,188	2,127	61	6,486	6,327	159
Chemicals-other	2,489	2,442	47	7,468	7,460	9
Newsprint	1,113	1,073	40	3,245	3,345	-101
Precious metals, other	554	519	35	1,720	1,953	-233
Fuel oil	2,945	2,912	33	9,081	14,340	-5,260
Chemicals-inorganic	745	712	33	2,172	2,257	-85
Cotton, raw	359	327	32	994	1,319	-326
Glass-plate, sheet, etc.	142	114	27	403	380	22
Tobacco, unmanufactured	127	100	27	319	299	20
Industrial rubber products	434	415	19	1,265	1,273	-8
Agric. farming-unmanufactured	281	262	19	814	853	-39
Hides and skins	223	206	16	630	792	-162
Electric energy	41	25	16	88	276	-188
Shingles, molding, wallboard	419	402	16	1,262	1,179	83
Copper	642	626	16	1,989	2,032	-43
Aluminum and alumina	700	686	14	2,052	2,148	-97
Leather and furs	122	111	11	335	331	4
Mineral supplies-manufactured	527	516	11	1,548	1,484	65
Nontextile floor tiles	52	44	8	145	155	-9
Manmade cloth	562	555	7	1,735	1,821	-86
Nonmetallic minerals	87	81	7	232	252	-21
Wood supplies, manufactured	112	106	7	332	367	-36
Hair, waste materials	56	54	3	164	159	6
Tapes, audio and visual	20	18	2	56	60	-4
Finished textile supplies	266	265	1	795	795	-1
Steelmaking materials	497	504	-7	1,662	2,169	-507
Cotton fiber cloth	198	207	-9	617	635	-18
Logs and lumber	525	540	-15	1,534	1,764	-231
Nonferrous metals, other	693	710	-17	2,092	2,050	41
Pulpwood and woodpulp	706	725	-19	2,189	2,250	-61
Natural gas liquids	674	704	-31	2,026	2,504	-478
Synthetic rubber-primary	268	312	-45	879	1,023	-144
Chemicals-organic	2,557	2,610	-53	7,648	7,554	94
Iron and steel mill products	853	910	-57	2,697	2,750	-53
Chemicals-fertilizers	713	796	-83	2,264	2,396	-131
Iron and steel products, other	597	701	-104	1,951	1,875	77
Nuclear fuel materials	125	303	-178	556	276	280
Coal and fuels, other	413	594	-181	1,439	1,810	-371
Petroleum products, other	3,483	4,148	-661	11,795	15,795	-4,000

Part A: Seasonally Adjusted (by Commodity/Service)

Exhibit 7. U.S. Exports of Goods by End-Use Category and Commodity

In millions of dollars. Details may not equal totals due to seasonal adjustment and rounding. The commodities in this exhibit are ranked on the monthly change within each major commodity grouping. (-) Represents zero or less than one-half of measurement shown. (R) - Revised.

Item (1)	March 2015	February 2015 (R)	Monthly Change	Year-to-Date 2015	Year-to-Date 2014	Year-to-Date Change
Capital goods, except automotive	**45,498**	**44,027**	**1,471**	**135,211**	**134,450**	**761**
Civilian aircraft	5,214	4,724	490	15,290	12,848	2,442
Engines-civilian aircraft	2,884	2,658	226	8,290	7,786	504
Electric apparatus	3,645	3,479	165	10,605	10,199	406
Telecommunications equipment	3,463	3,339	125	10,181	10,253	-72
Semiconductors	3,577	3,458	119	10,817	10,851	-35
Generators, accessories	1,173	1,067	106	3,383	3,418	-36
Railway transportation equipment	475	387	88	1,127	953	174
Agricultural machinery, equipment	631	555	77	1,754	2,163	-410
Laboratory testing instruments	938	882	56	2,788	2,755	34
Medicinal equipment	2,894	2,839	56	8,583	8,664	-82
Food, tobacco machinery	350	310	40	996	951	45
Computers	1,418	1,384	35	4,189	4,244	-54
Industrial machines, other	4,494	4,464	30	13,548	13,584	-37
Pulp and paper machinery	210	184	26	583	575	8
Wood, glass, plastic	363	337	26	1,041	977	64
Metalworking machine tools	655	634	21	1,926	1,759	167
Materials handling equipment	1,098	1,082	16	3,393	3,718	-325
Specialized mining	127	116	11	356	325	31
Marine engines, parts	130	123	7	380	326	53
Photo, service industry machinery	852	850	2	2,558	2,650	-92
Drilling & oilfield equipment	772	771	2	2,372	3,010	-638
Spacecraft, excluding military	4	3	1	17	11	6
Vessels, excluding scrap	2	2	0	8	99	-91
Textile, sewing machines	98	99	0	289	300	-11
Nonfarm tractors and parts	228	232	-4	681	833	-152
Business machines and equipment	232	243	-10	707	745	-38
Commercial vessels, other	22	40	-18	95	163	-68
Computer accessories	2,481	2,501	-19	7,504	8,165	-661
Measuring, testing, control instruments	2,026	2,058	-32	6,214	6,352	-138
Parts-civilian aircraft	1,759	1,808	-48	5,437	5,409	28
Excavating machinery	930	987	-58	2,942	3,315	-373
Industrial engines	2,352	2,413	-61	7,157	7,048	109
Automotive vehicles, parts, and engines	**12,282**	**11,490**	**792**	**36,318**	**37,165**	**-847**
Consumer goods	**16,141**	**17,839**	**-1,699**	**50,512**	**48,494**	**2,018**
Pharmaceutical preparations	4,336	5,091	-755	14,136	12,185	1,950
Artwork, antiques, stamps, etc.	791	1,059	-268	2,544	2,559	-15
Gem diamonds	1,789	2,050	-261	5,468	5,662	-194
Jewelry, etc.	1,096	1,334	-238	3,370	3,291	79
Cell phones and other household goods, n.e.c.	1,946	2,181	-234	6,305	5,972	333
Books, printed matter	369	416	-47	1,172	1,277	-105
Numismatic coins	54	77	-24	255	278	-22
Televisions and video equipment	366	383	-16	1,246	1,087	159
Musical instruments	139	155	-16	449	506	-57
Tobacco, manufactured	48	53	-5	149	138	11
Pleasure boats and motors	166	167	-1	521	567	-46
Glassware, chinaware	51	51	0	152	145	7
Toys, games, and sporting goods	809	808	1	2,436	2,553	-116
Cookware, cutlery, tools	99	98	1	290	280	10
Nursery stock, etc.	37	34	4	104	101	3
Rugs	93	89	4	275	278	-3
Other consumer nondurables	629	624	5	1,891	1,885	6
Furniture, household goods, etc.	419	414	5	1,266	1,220	46
Sports apparel and gear	69	61	8	196	201	-5
Household appliances	614	602	13	1,831	1,889	-58
Apparel, household goods-textile	590	573	17	1,747	1,691	57
Apparel, household goods-nontextile	268	250	18	768	715	53
Stereo equipment, etc.	167	148	19	475	513	-38
Recorded media	206	175	31	583	643	-59
Toiletries and cosmetics	986	946	40	2,882	2,857	25
Other goods	**4,694**	**4,658**	**36**	**13,862**	**14,407**	**-546**

(1) Detailed data are presented on a Census basis. The information needed to convert to a BOP basis is not available.

NOTE: For information on data sources, nonsampling errors, and definitions, see the information section on page A-1 of this release or at www.census.gov/ft900 or www.bea.gov/newsreleases/international/trade/tradnewsrelease.htm.

Part A: Seasonally Adjusted (by Commodity/Service)

Exhibit 8. U.S. Imports of Goods by End-Use Category and Commodity

In millions of dollars. Details may not equal totals due to seasonal adjustment and rounding. The commodities in this exhibit are ranked on the monthly change within each major commodity grouping (-) Represents zero or less than one-half of measurement shown. (R) - Revised.

Item (1)	March 2015	February 2015 (R)	Monthly Change	Year-to-Date 2015	Year-to-Date 2014	Year-to-Date Change
Total, Balance of Payments Basis	**197,630**	**181,268**	**16,361**	**569,970**	**581,712**	**-11,742**
Net Adjustments	1,837	1,919	-82	5,679	7,139	-1,460
Total, Census Basis	**195,793**	**179,350**	**16,443**	**564,290**	**574,573**	**-10,282**
Foods, feeds, and beverages	**11,027**	**10,301**	**726**	**31,955**	**29,820**	**2,136**
Fish and shellfish	1,878	1,655	223	5,251	5,289	-38
Green coffee	462	349	113	1,142	831	310
Feedstuff and foodgrains	545	466	79	1,561	1,590	-29
Nuts	243	172	72	617	507	109
Cane and beet sugar	188	118	70	431	365	66
Fruits, frozen juices	1,307	1,255	52	3,841	3,518	323
Tea, spices, etc.	219	175	43	565	496	69
Bakery products	785	760	25	2,316	2,267	49
Meat products	1,110	1,088	22	3,306	2,346	960
Other foods	1,043	1,022	20	3,175	3,145	30
Dairy products and eggs	196	169	17	519	435	83
Food oils, oilseeds	504	490	14	1,508	1,620	-112
Wine, beer, and related products	833	829	5	2,465	2,332	132
Alcoholic beverages, excluding wine	617	614	4	1,905	1,636	269
Nonagricultural foods, etc.	88	94	-6	278	253	25
Cocoa beans	147	157	-10	424	543	-119
Vegetables	873	889	-16	2,653	2,645	9
Industrial supplies and materials	**42,617**	**42,784**	**-167**	**132,391**	**172,618**	**-40,228**
Crude oil	10,612	11,434	-822	35,673	68,998	-33,325
Gas-natural	937	1,359	-422	3,102	3,469	-366
Petroleum products, other	2,380	2,612	-232	8,000	10,538	-2,538
Iron and steel mill products	1,992	2,188	-196	6,540	5,778	763
Electric energy	249	327	-78	758	887	-129
Steelmaking materials	520	595	-75	1,928	2,243	-315
Chemicals-organic	1,827	1,882	-55	5,935	6,991	-1,056
Fuel oil	2,171	2,220	-49	6,892	11,173	-4,280
Farming materials, livestock	97	135	-38	389	454	-65
Other precious metals	758	792	-34	2,434	2,685	-251
Tobacco, waxes etc.	742	760	-17	2,296	2,269	27
Coal and related fuels	131	148	-16	449	390	59
Chemicals-inorganic	663	677	-14	1,968	1,860	108
Sulfur, nonmetallic minerals	91	105	-14	325	338	-13
Zinc	114	125	-10	373	310	62
Nuclear fuel materials	116	123	-8	407	844	-437
Nonmonetary gold	911	916	-5	2,763	3,551	-789
Hides and skins	18	19	0	50	39	11
Wool, silk, etc.	72	72	0	205	200	6
Liquefied petroleum gases	206	205	1	717	1,499	-783
Cotton, natural fibers	8	6	2	18	18	0
Lumber	483	480	3	1,479	1,367	112
Tin	49	46	3	165	241	-75
Leather and furs	71	66	5	208	184	24
Hair, waste materials	91	83	8	262	240	22
Newsprint	111	95	16	304	353	-49
Blank tapes, audio & visual	63	46	17	163	180	-17
Materials, excluding chemicals	131	114	17	384	376	8
Natural rubber	125	105	20	367	586	-220
Synthetic rubber-primary	228	207	20	657	752	-95
Glass-plate, sheet, etc.	146	124	22	402	349	53
Nontextile floor tiles	283	260	24	820	779	41
Cotton cloth, fabrics	111	86	25	288	301	-14
Paper and paper products	661	632	28	1,919	1,840	78
Pulpwood and woodpulp	292	255	37	828	931	-103
Shingles, wallboard	823	781	42	2,429	2,217	212
Bauxite and aluminum	1,131	1,085	45	3,344	2,497	847
Iron and steel products, n.e.c.	878	829	49	2,672	2,360	312
Plywood and veneers	280	229	51	746	596	150
Synthetic cloth	558	507	51	1,621	1,537	84
Nickel	275	224	51	734	674	60
Nonferrous metals, other	339	315	53	1,010	1,096	-86
Chemicals-fertilizers	1,391	1,335	55	3,866	3,454	412
Finished textile supplies	438	368	70	1,207	1,169	38
Plastic materials	1,434	1,357	77	4,273	4,182	91
Stone, sand, cement, etc.	512	425	87	1,408	1,264	145
Chemicals-other, n.e.c.	1,082	988	94	3,095	2,986	109
Copper	462	358	104	1,326	1,162	164
Iron and steel, advanced	1,004	785	219	2,673	2,450	223
Finished metal shapes	1,644	1,377	267	4,517	4,500	17
Industrial supplies, other	2,879	2,521	358	8,002	7,464	538

Part A: Seasonally Adjusted (by Commodity/Service)

Exhibit 8. U.S. Imports of Goods by End-Use Category and Commodity

In millions of dollars. Details may not equal totals due to seasonal adjustment and rounding. The commodities in this exhibit are ranked on the monthly change within each major commodity grouping. (-) Represents zero or less than one-half of measurement shown. (R) - Revised.

Item (1)	March 2015	February 2015 (R)	Monthly Change	Year-to-Date 2015	Year-to-Date 2014	Year-to-Date Change
Capital goods, except automotive	**52,047**	**48,067**	**3,980**	**150,644**	**141,906**	**8,738**
Industrial machines, other	4,736	4,035	701	13,414	12,710	705
Computer accessories	5,266	4,720	546	14,997	14,208	789
Industrial engines	2,263	1,857	406	6,164	5,788	376
Electric apparatus	4,441	4,040	401	12,654	11,787	866
Telecommunications equipment	5,486	5,090	396	15,846	14,131	1,715
Generators, accessories	2,152	1,843	309	5,954	5,743	210
Semiconductors	3,795	3,500	295	10,756	10,425	331
Computers	4,721	4,483	237	14,259	14,635	-375
Photo, service industry machinery	1,636	1,419	217	4,559	4,303	256
Medicinal equipment	3,154	2,945	209	8,914	8,263	650
Metalworking machine tools	1,059	910	149	2,921	2,728	193
Business machines and equipment	531	385	146	1,304	1,216	88
Agricultural machinery, equipment	846	720	126	2,416	2,700	-284
Materials handling equipment	1,373	1,250	123	4,074	3,693	382
Wood, glass, plastic	699	579	120	1,909	1,855	53
Measuring, testing, control instruments	1,815	1,700	115	5,240	4,919	321
Food, tobacco machinery	331	280	51	912	887	26
Textile, sewing machines	214	176	38	589	530	59
Excavating machinery	1,011	977	33	3,127	2,645	482
Nonfarm tractors and parts	186	159	26	507	607	-100
Marine engines, parts	98	88	10	275	285	-10
Commercial vessels, other	12	6	6	25	19	6
Vessels, except scrap	0	0	0	1	1	0
Specialized mining	58	58	0	193	177	15
Railway transportation equipment	150	153	-3	444	364	81
Engines-civilian aircraft	1,613	1,618	-4	4,727	4,415	312
Spacecraft, excluding military	1	6	-5	10	19	-8
Laboratory testing instruments	477	483	-7	1,481	1,380	101
Pulp and paper machinery	377	385	-8	1,113	1,170	-56
Parts-civilian aircraft	1,424	1,447	-23	4,341	4,283	58
Drilling & oilfield equipment	856	898	-42	2,975	2,022	953
Civilian aircraft	1,267	1,854	-587	4,542	3,999	543
Automotive vehicles, parts, and engines	**28,851**	**26,185**	**2,666**	**82,838**	**77,182**	**5,655**
Consumer goods	**54,164**	**45,151**	**9,013**	**145,998**	**134,654**	**11,344**
Cell phones and other household goods, n.e.c.	9,106	7,428	1,677	24,795	21,049	3,745
Apparel, textiles, nonwool or cotton	5,019	3,726	1,293	12,475	10,990	1,485
Furniture, household goods, etc.	3,278	2,297	981	8,143	7,161	982
Apparel, household goods-cotton	4,498	3,770	728	11,988	12,245	-256
Footwear	2,285	1,675	609	5,514	5,107	407
Pharmaceutical preparations	8,844	8,255	589	24,988	21,774	3,215
Toys, games, and sporting goods	3,329	2,874	455	8,974	8,776	198
Televisions and video equipment	2,266	1,838	428	6,230	7,004	-775
Other consumer nondurables	1,470	1,137	333	3,782	3,485	297
Apparel, household goods-nontextile	1,057	741	316	2,547	2,283	265
Household appliances	2,189	1,879	311	6,257	5,977	280
Cookware, cutlery, tools	1,021	725	295	2,435	2,177	258
Camping apparel and gear	1,123	873	250	2,874	2,528	346
Stereo equipment, etc	614	453	161	1,541	1,631	-90
Motorcycles and parts	299	173	126	746	744	2
Gem stones, other	379	272	107	995	898	97
Books, printed matter	364	280	85	953	937	16
Glassware, chinaware	254	178	77	621	609	13
Pleasure boats and motors	254	188	66	893	632	262
Toiletries and cosmetics	896	835	61	2,582	2,509	73
Musical instruments	170	125	45	432	441	-9
Gem diamonds	2,039	1,999	39	5,946	5,919	27
Numismatic coins	146	111	35	366	484	-118
Rugs	225	202	23	634	598	36
Apparel, household goods-wool	313	293	20	868	895	-26
Nursery stock, etc.	147	147	0	424	411	13
Recorded media	61	66	-5	191	187	5
Artwork, antiques, stamps, etc.	1,058	1,069	-10	3,268	2,959	308
Photo equipment	274	289	-14	936	880	56
Jewelry	1,186	1,253	-67	3,599	3,365	233
Other goods	**7,086**	**6,862**	**224**	**20,465**	**18,392**	**2,073**

(1) Detailed data are presented on a Census basis. The information needed to convert to a BOP basis is not available.

NOTE: For information on data sources, nonsampling errors, and definitions, see the information section on page A-1 of this release or at www.census.gov/ft900 or www.bea.gov/newsreleases/international/trade/tradnewsrelease.htm.

Part A: Seasonally Adjusted (by Commodity/Service)

Exhibit 9. U.S. Trade in Petroleum and Non-Petroleum Products by End-Use

In millions of dollars. Details may not equal totals due to seasonal adjustment and rounding. (R) - Revised.

Period	Balance				Exports				Imports			
	Total	Net Adjust-ments	Petroleum (1)	Non-petroleum	Total	Net Adjust-ments	Petroleum (1)	Non-petroleum	Total	Net Adjust-ments	Petroleum (1)	Non-petroleum
2014												
Jan. - Dec.	-735,787	-14,210	-188,319	-533,258	1,635,133	11,936	145,695	1,477,502	2,370,920	26,146	334,014	2,010,760
Jan. - Mar.	-181,269	-4,177	-57,420	-119,672	400,442	2,962	34,788	362,692	581,712	7,139	92,208	482,365
January	-59,112	-670	-18,788	-39,654	133,863	1,594	12,245	120,024	192,975	2,264	31,033	159,678
February	-59,955	-2,205	-19,608	-38,142	130,669	190	11,071	119,409	190,624	2,395	30,679	157,551
March	-62,202	-1,301	-19,024	-41,876	135,910	1,179	11,472	123,259	198,112	2,480	30,496	165,136
April	-65,243	-925	-18,049	-46,270	135,398	1,205	11,791	122,401	200,641	2,130	29,840	168,671
May	-62,751	-868	-15,166	-46,716	137,235	1,267	13,164	122,804	199,986	2,135	28,330	169,520
June	-60,249	-970	-14,673	-44,605	136,987	1,155	12,709	123,123	197,236	2,126	27,382	167,728
July	-59,261	-883	-14,474	-43,904	139,341	1,271	13,843	124,227	198,602	2,155	28,317	168,130
August	-59,485	-1,254	-13,127	-45,104	139,296	787	14,136	124,373	198,781	2,041	27,262	169,478
September	-62,346	-1,395	-14,017	-46,934	136,354	759	12,353	123,241	198,700	2,154	26,370	170,176
October	-61,166	-1,120	-15,203	-44,843	138,954	950	10,988	127,017	200,120	2,070	26,190	171,860
November	-59,000	-1,073	-11,589	-46,339	136,909	1,049	11,634	124,225	195,909	2,123	23,223	170,564
December	-65,017	-1,544	-14,602	-48,871	134,217	530	10,289	123,398	199,234	2,074	24,891	172,269
2015												
Jan. - Mar.	-188,770	-2,920	-26,554	-159,295	381,200	2,759	24,728	353,712	569,970	5,679	51,283	513,008
January	-62,533	-1,014	-10,686	-50,833	128,539	909	8,757	118,872	191,072	1,924	19,443	169,705
February (R)	-55,677	-1,107	-8,198	-46,372	125,592	812	8,273	116,507	181,268	1,919	16,471	162,879
March	-70,561	-799	-7,671	-62,091	127,069	1,038	7,698	118,333	197,630	1,837	15,369	180,424
April												
May												
June												
July												
August												
September												
October												
November												
December												

(1) The petroleum products aggregated in the end-use commodity classification system include virtually the same energy-related petroleum products as those aggregated in the Standard International Trade Classification (SITC). The end-use petroleum products, however, include some products such as ethane, butane, benzene, and toluene, which are included in "Manufactured Goods" in the SITC.

NOTE: For information on data sources, nonsampling errors, definitions, and details concerning what is included in Net Adjustments, see the information section on page A-1 of this release or at www.census.gov/ft900 or www.bea.gov/newsreleases/international/trade/tradnewsrelease.htm.

Part A: Seasonally Adjusted (by Commodity/Service)

Exhibit 10. Real U.S. Trade in Goods by Principal End-Use Category
Chained (2009) Dollars

In millions of dollars. Details may not equal totals due to seasonal adjustment and rounding. The values in this exhibit are subject to periodic change, reflecting revisions to the source information for the monthly deflators. (-) Represents zero or less than one-half of measurement shown. (R) - Revised.

Period	Total Census Basis (1)	End-Use Commodity Category						
		Foods, Feeds, & Beverages	Industrial Supplies (2)	Capital Goods	Automotive Vehicles etc.	Consumer Goods	Other Goods	Residual (3)
Exports								
2014								
Jan. - Dec. (R)	1,448,042	108,461	399,932	545,702	152,304	193,813	55,501	-7,670
Jan. - Mar.	351,119	27,447	96,197	133,938	35,618	47,225	12,447	-1,754
January	117,327	9,234	33,464	44,398	11,652	14,943	3,873	-238
February	115,333	9,113	31,086	43,686	11,643	16,266	4,203	-664
March	118,459	9,100	31,647	45,854	12,323	16,016	4,371	-852
April	118,773	8,755	32,718	45,484	12,128	15,922	4,467	-701
May	120,120	8,769	32,806	45,228	12,859	16,325	4,873	-741
June	120,474	8,768	33,066	45,221	12,991	16,722	4,468	-761
July	122,176	8,356	33,829	45,747	14,555	15,976	4,557	-845
August	123,245	8,220	34,710	46,695	12,941	16,703	4,771	-794
September	121,106	9,314	33,323	45,511	12,833	16,086	4,654	-615
October (R)	124,405	9,592	33,863	47,176	12,988	16,587	4,904	-704
November (R)	123,531	9,706	35,369	44,934	12,520	16,191	5,083	-274
December (R)	123,093	9,533	34,050	45,766	12,871	16,076	5,277	-480
2015								
Jan. - Mar.	356,499	26,868	100,092	133,681	34,676	50,015	12,808	-1,642
January (R)	120,114	8,816	34,230	45,217	11,967	16,282	4,163	-562
February (R)	117,540	8,826	32,816	43,492	10,982	17,694	4,304	-575
March	118,845	9,227	33,046	44,972	11,727	16,039	4,341	-506
April								
May								
June								
July								
August								
September								
October								
November								
December								
Imports								
2014								
Jan. - Dec. (R)	2,047,020	97,437	465,197	604,436	313,342	538,982	71,832	-44,205
Jan. - Mar.	497,953	23,376	117,353	145,308	73,609	130,322	17,021	-9,036
January	165,682	7,726	39,210	48,786	24,234	43,287	5,426	-2,988
February	163,335	7,559	38,965	47,603	24,352	42,159	5,484	-2,788
March	168,936	8,091	39,178	48,918	25,023	44,876	6,111	-3,260
April	172,451	8,291	39,765	49,741	25,849	45,786	6,411	-3,391
May	171,949	8,260	38,518	50,671	27,143	45,457	5,800	-3,901
June	169,096	8,576	37,829	50,415	26,139	44,044	5,880	-3,786
July	169,610	8,435	37,530	50,107	27,682	43,519	6,291	-3,954
August	171,124	8,109	38,524	51,950	26,337	44,183	5,943	-3,922
September	171,582	8,218	38,203	51,029	25,850	46,055	6,232	-4,006
October (R)	174,033	8,291	39,152	52,020	27,086	45,434	6,000	-3,950
November (R)	172,058	7,946	37,400	51,673	26,424	47,154	5,881	-4,419
December (R)	177,163	7,934	40,923	51,523	27,223	47,027	6,372	-3,839
2015								
Jan. - Mar.	529,625	24,895	119,611	154,960	80,366	141,973	19,258	-11,437
January (R)	174,869	8,324	40,010	51,902	26,898	45,425	6,111	-3,801
February (R)	168,716	7,922	39,174	49,471	25,407	43,878	6,448	-3,584
March	186,040	8,649	40,427	53,587	28,061	52,669	6,699	-4,053
April								
May								
June								
July								
August								
September								
October								
November								
December								

(1) Detailed data are presented on a Census basis. The information needed to convert to a BOP basis is not available.
(2) Includes petroleum and petroleum products.
(3) The "residual" represents the difference between total exports or imports of goods on a Census basis and the sum of the components. For additional information, see www.census.gov/foreign-trade/aip/priceadj.html.

NOTE: For information on data sources, nonsampling errors, and definitions, see the information section on page A-1 of this release or at www.census.gov/ft900 or www.bea.gov/newsreleases/international/trade/tradnewsrelease.htm.

Part A: Seasonally Adjusted (by Commodity/Service)

Exhibit 11. Real U.S. Trade in Petroleum and Non-Petroleum Products by End-Use
Chained (2009) Dollars

In millions of dollars. Details may not equal totals due to seasonal adjustment and rounding. The values in this exhibit are subject to periodic change, reflecting revisions to the source information for the monthly deflators. (-) Represents zero or less than one-half of measurement shown. (R) - Revised.

Period	Balance				Exports				Imports			
	Total Census Basis (1)	Petroleum	Non-petroleum	Residual (2)	Total Census Basis (1)	Petroleum	Non-petroleum	Residual (2)	Total Census Basis (1)	Petroleum	Non-petroleum	Residual (2)
2013												
Jan. - Dec.	-570,956	-132,201	-490,474	51,719	1,398,203	83,155	1,305,945	9,104	1,969,159	215,356	1,796,420	-42,616
Jan. - Mar.	-143,272	-37,042	-116,678	10,449	340,310	17,669	321,853	1,088	483,881	54,711	438,552	-9,361
January	-49,461	-13,241	-39,287	3,067	113,258	5,675	107,323	260	162,719	18,916	146,610	-2,807
February	-48,844	-11,829	-40,912	3,896	113,796	6,249	107,002	545	162,640	18,078	147,913	-3,351
March	-44,966	-11,972	-36,479	3,486	113,356	5,745	107,529	282	158,522	17,718	144,008	-3,204
April	-47,204	-11,874	-39,141	3,811	115,179	6,082	108,685	411	162,383	17,956	147,826	-3,399
May	-51,932	-12,370	-43,419	3,858	115,080	6,533	107,934	614	167,012	18,903	151,353	-3,244
June	-44,458	-10,367	-38,554	4,463	118,055	7,253	109,937	866	162,513	17,620	148,491	-3,598
July	-47,357	-10,538	-41,334	4,514	117,173	7,509	108,665	999	164,530	18,046	149,999	-3,516
August	-47,653	-10,358	-41,971	4,676	117,054	7,347	108,785	922	164,707	17,705	150,756	-3,754
September	-50,401	-10,952	-43,989	4,540	116,332	6,983	108,601	748	166,733	17,935	152,590	-3,793
October	-46,499	-10,246	-41,056	4,803	120,519	7,827	111,617	1,074	167,018	18,074	152,673	-3,728
November	-45,117	-9,260	-41,139	5,282	120,414	7,870	111,447	1,098	165,531	17,130	152,585	-4,184
December	-47,063	-9,194	-43,193	5,323	117,787	8,081	108,421	1,285	164,851	17,275	151,614	-4,038
2014												
Jan. - Dec. (R)	-598,977	-114,074	-550,888	65,985	1,448,042	91,610	1,345,912	10,521	2,047,020	205,684	1,896,800	-55,465
Jan. - Mar.	-146,834	-34,187	-125,098	12,451	351,119	20,032	329,600	1,487	497,953	54,219	454,697	-10,963
January	-48,356	-11,043	-41,632	4,319	117,327	7,118	109,467	742	165,682	18,161	151,099	-3,577
February	-48,002	-11,764	-39,992	3,754	115,333	6,346	108,634	353	163,335	18,110	148,626	-3,401
March	-50,477	-11,380	-43,474	4,377	118,459	6,568	111,499	392	168,936	17,948	154,972	-3,985
April	-53,678	-10,634	-48,111	5,067	118,773	7,255	110,771	747	172,451	17,889	158,882	-4,320
May	-51,829	-8,919	-48,814	5,904	120,120	8,020	111,019	1,081	171,949	16,939	159,833	-4,823
June	-48,622	-8,177	-46,557	6,113	120,474	7,831	111,660	983	169,096	16,008	158,218	-5,130
July	-47,435	-7,820	-45,868	6,253	122,176	8,442	112,498	1,236	169,610	16,261	158,366	-5,017
August	-47,879	-7,737	-46,507	6,365	123,245	8,803	113,060	1,383	171,124	16,540	159,566	-4,982
September	-50,476	-8,559	-48,009	6,092	121,106	7,763	112,388	955	171,582	16,321	160,397	-5,137
October (R)	-49,628	-9,693	-45,629	5,694	124,405	7,176	116,590	640	174,033	16,869	162,218	-5,055
November (R)	-48,528	-7,774	-47,069	6,315	123,531	8,172	114,349	1,009	172,058	15,946	161,418	-5,306
December (R)	-54,069	-10,574	-49,228	5,733	123,093	8,117	113,977	999	177,163	18,691	163,206	-4,734
2015												
Jan. - Mar.	-173,126	-29,530	-160,896	17,300	356,499	22,955	330,552	2,992	529,625	52,486	491,447	-14,308
January (R)	-54,755	-9,137	-51,428	5,810	120,114	8,509	110,593	1,012	174,869	17,645	162,021	-4,798
February (R)	-51,176	-9,896	-46,918	5,638	117,540	7,608	108,932	1,000	168,716	17,505	155,850	-4,638
March	-67,195	-10,497	-62,550	5,852	118,845	6,838	111,026	980	186,040	17,336	173,576	-4,872
April												
May												
June												
July												
August												
September												
October												
November												
December												

(1) Detailed data are presented on a Census basis. The information needed to convert to a BOP basis is not available.
(2) The "residual" represents the difference between total exports or imports of goods on a Census basis and the sum of the components. For additional information, see www.census.gov/foreign-trade/aip/priceadj.html.

NOTE: For information on data sources, nonsampling errors, and definitions, see the information section on page A-1 of this release or at www.census.gov/ft900 or www.bea.gov/newsreleases/international/trade/tradnewsrelease.htm.

Part B: NOT Seasonally Adjusted

Exhibit 12. U.S. Trade in Goods

In millions of dollars. Details may not equal totals due to rounding. (R) - Revised.

Period	Balance		Exports			Imports		
	Total Balance of Payments Basis	Total Census Basis	Total Balance of Payments Basis	Net Adjustments	Total Census Basis	Total Balance of Payments Basis	Net Adjustments	Total Census Basis
2013								
Jan. - Dec.	-701,669	-688,728	1,592,784	13,191	1,579,593	2,294,453	26,131	2,268,321
Jan. - Mar.	-156,922	-153,975	386,924	3,496	383,428	543,846	6,443	537,403
January	-62,670	-62,060	124,580	1,450	123,130	187,250	2,060	185,190
February	-48,176	-46,822	124,407	871	123,536	172,583	2,225	170,358
March	-46,077	-45,093	137,937	1,174	136,762	184,013	2,158	181,855
April	-62,199	-61,096	130,494	1,030	129,465	192,693	2,132	190,561
May	-64,719	-63,679	133,996	989	133,007	198,715	2,029	196,686
June	-51,520	-50,135	135,481	652	134,830	187,001	2,037	184,965
July	-71,010	-70,026	128,569	1,211	127,358	199,578	2,194	197,384
August	-61,475	-60,506	133,942	1,338	132,604	195,417	2,306	193,110
September	-64,456	-63,453	129,653	1,138	128,515	194,109	2,141	191,968
October	-64,234	-62,916	143,121	939	142,182	207,355	2,256	205,098
November	-53,343	-52,432	137,575	1,326	136,249	190,919	2,238	188,681
December	-51,791	-50,509	133,029	1,073	131,956	184,820	2,355	182,465
2014								
Jan. - Dec.	-735,787	-721,577	1,635,133	11,936	1,623,197	2,370,920	26,146	2,344,774
Jan. - Mar.	-158,774	-154,572	395,987	2,846	393,141	554,761	7,048	547,713
January	-57,873	-57,193	129,057	1,549	127,508	186,930	2,229	184,701
February	-48,104	-45,937	123,861	133	123,728	171,966	2,301	169,665
March	-52,797	-51,441	143,069	1,164	141,905	195,866	2,519	193,346
April	-67,610	-66,700	135,050	1,233	133,817	202,660	2,143	200,517
May	-62,701	-61,852	139,517	1,292	138,225	202,218	2,141	200,077
June	-59,997	-59,046	139,573	1,173	138,400	199,569	2,123	197,446
July	-71,622	-70,762	134,799	1,308	133,491	206,421	2,169	204,253
August	-59,947	-58,657	138,700	822	137,878	198,647	2,112	196,536
September	-70,802	-69,389	134,173	748	133,425	204,975	2,161	202,814
October	-66,087	-64,907	146,788	959	145,829	212,875	2,139	210,736
November	-55,670	-54,603	136,212	1,021	135,191	191,881	2,088	189,794
December	-62,577	-61,088	134,334	534	133,800	196,911	2,023	194,888
2015								
Jan. - Mar.	-169,753	-166,789	375,737	2,666	373,071	545,490	5,630	539,860
January	-59,739	-58,716	122,270	872	121,398	182,009	1,896	180,113
February (R)	-44,983	-43,899	119,114	766	118,348	164,097	1,850	162,246
March	-65,031	-64,175	134,353	1,028	133,325	199,385	1,884	197,500
April								
May								
June								
July								
August								
September								
October								
November								
December								

February data as published last month:

	-44,586	-43,495	119,168	814	118,354	163,754	1,906	161,849

NOTE: For information on data sources, nonsampling errors, definitions, and details concerning what is included in Net Adjustments, see the information section on page A-1 of this release or at www.census.gov/ft900 or www.bea.gov/newsreleases/international/trade/tradnewsrelease.htm.

Part B: NOT Seasonally Adjusted

Exhibit 13. U.S. Trade in Goods by Principal End-Use Category

In millions of dollars. Details may not equal totals due to rounding. (R) - Revised.

Period	Total Balance of Payments Basis	Net Adjustments	Total Census Basis (1)	End-Use Commodity Category					
				Foods, Feeds, & Beverages	Industrial Supplies (2)	Capital Goods	Automotive Vehicles, etc.	Consumer Goods	Other Goods
Exports									
2014									
Jan. - Dec.	1,635,133	11,936	1,623 197	144,171	506,831	550,046	159,453	199,150	63,545
Jan. - Mar.	395,987	2,846	393 141	37,897	125,767	130,697	36,484	47,952	14,345
January	129,057	1,549	127 508	13,077	43,390	41,622	10,430	14,583	4,406
February	123,861	133	123 728	12,205	38,777	40,109	11,834	15,985	4,818
March	143,069	1,164	141 905	12,615	43,599	48,966	14,219	17,384	5,121
April	135,050	1,233	133 817	11,406	42,649	45,132	13,382	16,105	5,143
May	139,517	1,292	138 225	11,124	43,576	46,528	14,455	16,900	5,642
June	139,573	1,173	138 400	10,425	42,400	47,270	14,228	18,908	5,169
July	134,799	1,308	133 491	10,279	43,557	45,710	12,914	15,768	5,262
August	138,700	822	137 878	10,242	44,563	47,258	13,745	16,570	5,499
September	134,173	748	133 425	10,492	41,369	45,638	13,764	16,841	5,321
October	146,788	959	145 829	14,524	43,363	49,619	14,559	18,176	5,589
November	136,212	1,021	135 191	14,606	40,464	44,606	13,312	16,501	5,702
December	134,334	534	133 800	13,176	39,125	47,588	12,610	15,428	5,873
2015									
Jan. - Mar.	375,737	2,666	373 071	33,827	109,013	131,079	35,475	49,887	13,790
January	122,270	872	121 398	11,657	36,439	42,593	10,705	15,556	4,448
February (R)	119,114	766	118 348	10,831	34,322	40,271	11,179	17,135	4,610
March	134,353	1,028	133 325	11,339	38,253	48,216	13,590	17,196	4,732
April									
May									
June									
July									
August									
September									
October									
November									
December									
Imports									
2014									
Jan. - Dec.	2,370,920	26,146	2,344 774	125,718	665,164	591,001	327,645	557,696	77,550
Jan. - Mar.	554,761	7,048	547 713	29,749	165,611	134,696	75,305	124,150	18,201
January	186,930	2,229	184 701	9,956	56,767	45,111	23,236	43,814	5,817
February	171,966	2,301	169 665	8,826	51,045	41,191	24,288	38,889	5,426
March	195,866	2,519	193 346	10,967	57,798	48,394	27,782	41,447	6,959
April	202,660	2,143	200 517	10,952	60,417	48,629	27,799	45,567	7,152
May	202,218	2,141	200 077	10,968	58,433	49,935	28,121	46,377	6,242
June	199,569	2,123	197 446	10,874	56,485	51,201	27,817	44,575	6,494
July	206,421	2,169	204 253	10,762	59,737	51,248	27,376	48,259	6,872
August	198,647	2,112	196 536	10,076	56,223	49,776	27,950	46,491	6,020
September	204,975	2,161	202 814	10,135	55,257	50,900	27,000	52,497	7,025
October	212,875	2,139	210 736	11,170	55,228	53,167	30,273	54,064	6,834
November	191,881	2,088	189 794	10,107	46,715	49,846	28,182	48,995	5,949
December	196,911	2,023	194 888	10,925	51,058	51,603	27,821	46,721	6,760
2015									
Jan. - Mar.	545,490	5,630	539 860	31,900	128,398	143,541	80,713	135,043	20,264
January	182,009	1,896	180 113	10,728	46,020	47,080	25,012	44,935	6,339
February (R)	164,097	1,850	162 246	9,513	38,624	42,655	24,840	40,379	6,235
March	199,385	1,884	197 500	11,659	43,754	53,807	30,862	49,729	7,690
April									
May									
June									
July									
August									
September									
October									
November									
December									

(1) Detailed data are presented on a Census basis. The information needed to convert to a BOP basis is not available.
(2) Includes petroleum and petroleum products.

NOTE: For information on data sources, nonsampling errors, and definitions, see the information section on page A-1 of this release or at www.census.gov/ft900 or www.bea.gov/newsreleases/international/trade/tradnewsrelease.htm.

Part B: NOT Seasonally Adjusted

Exhibit 14. U.S. Trade in Goods by Selected Countries and Areas: 2015

In millions of dollars. Details may not equal totals due to rounding. (-) Represents zero or less than one-half of measurement shown.
(R) - Revised. (X) - Not applicable.

Item (1)	Balance			Exports			Imports		
	March 2015	February 2015	Year-to-Date 2015	March 2015	February 2015	Year-to-Date 2015	March 2015	February 2015	Year-to-Date 2015
Total Balance of Payments Basis	**-65,031** (R)	**-44,983**	**-169,753**	**134,353** (R)	**119,114**	**375,737**	**199,385** (R)	**164,097**	**545,490**
Net Adjustments	-856 (R)	-1,084	-2,964	1,028 (R)	766	2,666	1,884 (R)	1,850	5,630
Total Census Basis	**-64,175** (R)	**-43,899**	**-166,789**	**133,325** (R)	**118,348**	**373,071**	**197,500** (R)	**162,246**	**539,860**
North America	-6,262 (R)	-5,758	-17,879	44,904 (R)	39,976	126,487	51,166	45,734	144,366
Canada	-762 (R)	-1,409	-5,112	25,035 (R)	21,849	69,347	25,797	23,258	74,459
Mexico	-5,500	-4,349	-12,767	19,870	18,127	57,140	25,369	22,476	69,907
Europe	-13,390	-10,399	-34,223	29,569	26,019	81,789	42,959	36,418	116,012
European Union	-12,669	-9,334	-31,326	24,188	22,269	68,723	36,858	31,603	100,049
Austria	-818	169	-688	215	1,036	2,043	1,033	867	2,731
Belgium	1,281	1,124	3,918	2,917	2,651	8,447	1,636	1,527	4,528
Czech Republic	-210	-187	-602	174	150	498	385	336	1,099
Finland	-278	-223	-766	125	98	380	403	321	1,146
France	-1,568	-1,101	-3,594	2,594	2,385	7,556	4,162	3,486	11,150
Germany	-6,095	-5,306	-16,699	4,667	4,072	12,483	10,762	9,377	29,181
Hungary	-414	-320	-1,025	145	154	434	559	474	1,459
Ireland	-2,327	-1,977	-6,659	899	739	2,258	3,225	2,715	8,917
Italy	-2,275	-2,131	-6,427	1,541	1,178	3,940	3,816	3,308	10,367
Netherlands	2,311	2,019	5,966	3,880	3,295	10,404	1,569	1,276	4,438
Poland	-56	-97	-242	439	281	1,020	495	378	1,262
Spain	-462	-175	-764	763	798	2,479	1,225	973	3,243
Sweden	-519	-374	-1,312	347	338	980	866	712	2,293
United Kingdom	-31	60	281	4,546	4,381	13,350	4,577	4,320	13,069
Other	-1,208	-817	-2,714	935	713	2,451	2,143	1,530	5,165
Norway	7	-109	-139	393	270	905	386	379	1,044
Russia	-867	-798	-2,591	702	585	1,932	1,569	1,383	4,523
Switzerland	-373	-393	-1,234	2,763	1,662	6,116	3,137	2,055	7,350
Other Europe	513	236	1,067	1,523	1,232	4,113	1,010	997	3,045
Euro Area	-10,638	-7,899	-26,566	18,203	16,683	51,493	28,841	24,581	78,059
Pacific Rim Countries	-41,150	-26,422	-104,451	32,537	28,590	90,744	73,687	55,012	195,195
Australia	1,246	965	3,309	2,162	1,789	5,926	915	824	2,617
China	-31,235	-22,540	-82,381	9,887	8,700	28,139	41,122	31,240	110,520
Indonesia	-1,016	-696	-2,790	733	605	1,917	1,748	1,301	4,708
Japan	-7,125	-4,182	-17,073	5,717	5,040	15,874	12,842	9,222	32,947
Malaysia	-1,728	-1,331	-4,679	1,167	916	3,049	2,895	2,247	7,728
Philippines	-343	-54	-548	676	605	1,971	1,019	658	2,519
Newly Industrialized Countries	-841	1,456	-112	11,814	10,640	32,856	12,655	9,184	32,968
Hong Kong	2,274	3,139	7,910	3,089	3,498	9,451	815	360	1,541
Korea, South	-2,200	-1,652	-6,920	4,062	3,310	10,690	6,263	4,962	17,611
Singapore	1,249	943	3,228	2,704	2,027	7,033	1,455	1,084	3,805
Taiwan	-2,164	-973	-4,329	1,959	1,805	5,683	4,123	2,779	10,012
Other	-110	-40	-178	381	294	1,010	491	335	1,188
South/Central America	3,009	3,446	8,541	13,767	12,515	39,032	10,759	9,069	30,491
Argentina	506	422	1,253	842	676	2,205	336	253	952
Brazil	600	797	1,764	2,805	2,837	8,475	2,205	2,041	6,711
Chile	423	644	1,259	1,439	1,485	4,092	1,016	841	2,833
Colombia	24	308	484	1,523	1,235	4,137	1,499	927	3,654
Other	1,455	1,275	3,781	7,158	6,281	20,122	5,703	5,007	16,341
OPEC	1,154	719	751	6,407	5,832	17,854	5,253	5,114	17,103
Nigeria	192	267	544	287	327	844	95	60	300
Saudi Arabia	185	-279	-721	1,748	1,270	4,545	1,562	1,548	5,266
Venezuela	-657	-532	-2,074	793	606	2,093	1,449	1,138	4,166
Other	1,433	1,262	3,001	3,580	3,629	10,372	2,147	2,367	7,371
Africa	133	249	448	2,190	2,002	6,407	2,058	1,753	5,959
Algeria	-2	-155	-278	151	103	403	153	258	681
Egypt	241	249	727	363	373	1,093	122	124	366
South Africa	-119	-23	-385	482	394	1,352	601	417	1,737
Other	12	178	384	1,193	1,133	3,559	1,181	955	3,174
Other Countries	-8,402	-6,080	-21,839	5,810	5,040	15,846	14,211	11,120	37,685
India	-2,303	-1,648	-6,041	1,790	1,663	4,998	4,094	3,312	11,039
Thailand	-1,503	-1,142	-3,799	1,115	775	2,947	2,618	1,917	6,746
Other	-4,595	-3,289	-11,999	2,905	2,602	7,901	7,500	5,891	19,900
Unidentified Countries (2)	(-)	(-)	(-)	(-)	(-)	(-)	(X)	(X)	(X)
Timing Adjustments	(X)	-390	-1,056	(X)	7	43	(X)	397	1,098

(1) Detailed data are presented on a Census basis. The information needed to convert to a BOP basis is not available.
(2) The export totals reflect shipments of certain grains, oilseeds, and satellites that are not included in the country/area totals.

NOTES:
* This exhibit is not additive; countries may be included in more than one area. For a list of countries in each area, see the information section on page A-2 of this release or at www.census.gov/ft900 or www.bea.gov/newsreleases/international/trade/tradnewsrelease.htm.
* Area data reflect the composition of the areas as they were at the time of reporting.
* For information on data sources, nonsampling errors, and definitions, see the information section on page A-1 of this release or at www.census.gov/ft900 or www.bea.gov/newsreleases/international/trade/tradnewsrelease.htm.

Part B: NOT Seasonally Adjusted

Exhibit 14a. U.S. Trade in Goods by Selected Countries and Areas: 2014

In millions of dollars. Details may not equal totals due to rounding. (-) Represents zero or less than one-half of measurement shown. (X) - Not applicable.

Item (1)	Balance			Exports			Imports		
	March 2014	February 2014	Year-to-Date 2014	March 2014	February 2014	Year-to-Date 2014	March 2014	February 2014	Year-to-Date 2014
Total Balance of Payments Basis	**-52,797**	**-48,104**	**-158,774**	**143,069**	**123,861**	**395,987**	**195,866**	**171,966**	**554,761**
Net Adjustments	-1,355	-2,167	-4,202	1,164	133	2,846	2,519	2,301	7,048
Total Census Basis	**-51,441**	**-45,937**	**-154,572**	**141,905**	**123,728**	**393,141**	**193,346**	**169,665**	**547,713**
North America	-7,337	-6,118	-20,261	47,045	41,603	130,453	54,381	47,721	150,713
Canada	-2,278	-2,146	-8,473	27,148	23,255	73,061	29,426	25,401	81,534
Mexico	-5,059	-3,972	-11,788	19,897	18,348	57,392	24,956	22,321	69,180
Europe	-12,383	-9,085	-31,612	30,644	26,450	82,979	43,027	35,535	114,591
European Union	-11,506	-9,083	-29,397	24,566	20,961	67,023	36,072	30,045	96,419
Austria	-774	-266	-1,327	204	490	1,134	978	757	2,461
Belgium	1,236	1,161	3,579	3,073	2,639	8,302	1,837	1,478	4,724
Czech Republic	-177	-124	-431	175	189	532	352	314	963
Finland	-277	-117	-523	198	181	555	475	297	1,078
France	-1,650	-1,416	-3,968	2,598	2,331	7,494	4,248	3,747	11,462
Germany	-5,909	-4,532	-15,646	4,659	4,355	12,883	10,568	8,887	28,529
Hungary	-235	-174	-614	208	150	494	443	324	1,109
Ireland	-1,812	-1,861	-5,421	736	521	1,830	2,548	2,382	7,251
Italy	-1,707	-1,528	-5,041	1,851	1,317	4,430	3,558	2,846	9,470
Netherlands	1,770	1,518	5,127	3,727	3,125	10,217	1,957	1,608	5,089
Poland	-114	-91	-307	332	275	879	447	366	1,186
Spain	-408	-177	-638	810	777	2,534	1,218	954	3,172
Sweden	-429	-437	-1,158	416	313	1,054	845	750	2,212
United Kingdom	-182	-311	-732	4,521	3,564	11,994	4,703	3,875	12,726
Other	-839	-728	-2,297	1,057	732	2,689	1,896	1,460	4,986
Norway	-343	143	-287	371	529	1,295	714	386	1,582
Russia	-1,535	-949	-3,481	1,013	928	2,832	2,548	1,877	6,313
Switzerland	120	51	-749	2,783	2,402	6,661	2,663	2,350	7,410
Other Europe	880	753	2,302	1,912	1,630	5,169	1,031	877	2,867
Euro Area	-9,754	-7,385	-24,361	18,415	16,117	50,875	28,169	23,502	75,235
Pacific Rim Countries	-25,737	-24,018	-81,720	34,802	30,931	98,920	60,539	54,949	180,639
Australia	1,343	1,422	4,133	2,133	2,089	6,383	790	668	2,250
China	-20,404	-20,862	-69,105	10,830	9,879	31,066	31,234	30,741	100,171
Indonesia	-1,126	-687	-2,832	685	721	2,052	1,810	1,407	4,884
Japan	-5,942	-5,261	-16,526	6,026	5,328	16,900	11,968	10,589	33,426
Malaysia	-1,214	-1,058	-3,515	1,181	941	3,047	2,395	1,998	6,563
Philippines	-86	-84	-196	799	608	2,170	885	691	2,366
Newly Industrialized Countries	1,502	2,545	6,201	12,610	11,107	36,228	11,108	8,562	30,027
Hong Kong	2,373	2,949	9,235	3,306	3,187	10,850	933	238	1,615
Korea, South	-1,256	-1,035	-4,174	4,364	3,525	11,357	5,619	4,560	15,531
Singapore	1,335	1,263	4,178	2,590	2,372	7,734	1,255	1,109	3,557
Taiwan	-949	-632	-3,037	2,351	2,023	6,287	3,301	2,655	9,324
Other	189	-34	121	537	259	1,073	348	292	953
South/Central America	3,317	1,279	7,348	16,042	13,315	44,696	12,725	12,036	37,348
Argentina	437	587	1,712	850	875	2,629	413	288	917
Brazil	1,837	1,196	4,282	3,943	3,282	10,745	2,107	2,086	6,464
Chile	469	388	1,374	1,454	1,134	3,979	984	746	2,606
Colombia	45	-240	-196	1,746	1,312	4,864	1,701	1,553	5,060
Other	529	-652	177	8,049	6,712	22,478	7,520	7,363	22,301
OPEC	-5,193	-5,741	-17,933	6,663	5,759	18,343	11,855	11,499	36,276
Nigeria	-182	252	53	453	519	1,338	635	267	1,285
Saudi Arabia	-3,250	-3,225	-10,350	1,632	1,249	4,099	4,882	4,474	14,450
Venezuela	-1,821	-1,774	-5,936	697	599	1,979	2,518	2,372	7,914
Other	61	-994	-1,700	3,881	3,392	10,926	3,820	4,386	12,627
Africa	-40	115	170	3,025	2,842	8,625	3,065	2,727	8,455
Algeria	-112	-145	-194	208	209	787	320	354	981
Egypt	577	470	1,259	704	563	1,607	126	93	348
South Africa	-95	-201	-380	576	437	1,535	672	638	1,915
Other	-409	-9	-515	1,538	1,634	4,696	1,947	1,643	5,212
Other Countries	-5,783	-5,584	-18,029	5,830	4,714	15,651	11,613	10,298	33,680
India	-2,168	-1,676	-5,937	1,714	1,367	4,664	3,882	3,043	10,601
Thailand	-1,262	-1,000	-3,253	1,042	799	2,984	2,304	1,799	6,237
Other	-2,353	-2,908	-8,839	3,074	2,548	8,003	5,427	5,456	16,842
Unidentified Countries (2)	(-)	(-)	(-)	(-)	(-)	(-)	(X)	(X)	(X)

(1) Detailed data are presented on a Census basis. The information needed to convert to a BOP basis is not available.
(2) The export totals reflect shipments of certain grains, oilseeds, and satellites that are not included in the country/area totals.

NOTES:
* This exhibit is not additive; countries may be included in more than one area. For a list of countries in each area, see the information section on page A-2 of this release or at www.census.gov/ft900 or www.bea.gov/newsreleases/international/trade/tradnewsrelease.htm.
* Area data reflect the composition of the areas as they were at the time of reporting.
* For information on data sources, nonsampling errors, and definitions, see the information section on page A-1 of this release or at www.census.gov/ft900 or www.bea.gov/newsreleases/international/trade/tradnewsrelease.htm.

Part B: NOT Seasonally Adjusted

Exhibit 15. U.S. Trade in Goods by Principal Commodities

In millions of dollars. Details may not equal totals due to rounding. This exhibit is not additive.
(R) - Revised. (X) - Not applicable. (-) Represents zero or less than one-half of measurement shown.

Item (1)	2015						2014	
	March		February		Year-to-Date		Year-to-Date	
	Exports	Imports	Exports	Imports	Exports	Imports	Exports	Imports
Total Balance of Payment Basis (2)	**134,353**	**199,385**	(R) **119,114**	(R) **164,097**	**375,737**	**545,490**	**395,987**	**554,761**
Net Adjustments (2)	1,028	1,884	(R) 766	(R) 1,850	2,666	5,630	2,846	7,048
Total Census Basis (2)	**133,325**	**197,500**	(R) **118,348**	(R) **162,246**	**373,071**	**539,860**	**393,141**	**547,713**
Manufactured Goods (3)	99,219	171,179	85,985	138,273	273,957	461,033	286,901	440,186
Agricultural Commodities (3)	12,175	10,616	11,508	8,734	35,973	28,860	40,925	27,183
Food and Live Animals	**9,225**	**9,150**	**7,902**	**7,539**	**24,609**	**25,202**	**26,139**	**23,498**
Live animals other than fish	53	365	51	291	147	893	169	790
Meat and preparations	1,431	963	1,353	752	4,125	2,607	4,437	1,731
Dairy products and birds' eggs	482	191	379	154	1,211	490	1,660	414
Fish and preparations	521	1,551	377	1,345	1,117	4,605	1,105	4,671
Cereals and preparations	2,191	814	2,068	641	6,134	2,167	6,521	2,166
Vegetables and fruit	2,163	2,957	1,653	2,520	5,344	8,346	5,071	7,862
Sugars, preparations and honey	173	422	141	321	471	1,083	569	1,011
Coffee, tea, cocoa and spices	251	1,261	224	994	711	3,272	717	3,059
Feeding stuff for animals	1,193	227	985	213	3,240	693	3,739	761
Miscellaneous edible products	766	399	669	308	2,109	1,045	2,150	1,032
Beverages and Tobacco	**715**	**1,988**	**545**	**1,499**	**1,696**	**5,106**	**1,633**	**4,706**
Beverages	435	1,814	371	1,326	1,115	4,630	1,098	4,209
Tobacco and manufactures	281	174	174	172	581	475	535	497
Crude Materials Except Fuels	**5,914**	**2,816**	**6,516**	**2,586**	**20,024**	**8,270**	**24,499**	**8,798**
Hides, skins and furskins, raw	267	26	206	46	667	105	836	125
Oil seeds and oleaginous fruits	1,208	145	2,197	122	6,738	382	9,579	428
Crude rubber	218	286	250	208	690	767	830	1,065
Cork and wood	603	639	552	532	1,631	1,730	1,830	1,586
Pulp and waste paper	707	296	655	248	2,092	799	2,135	897
Textile fibers, including waste	725	122	662	104	1,982	359	2,494	332
Crude fertilizers	229	222	220	224	640	712	632	679
Metalliferous ores and metal scrap	1,634	553	1,505	582	4,732	1,815	5,332	2,118
Crude animal and vegetable materials	323	526	269	519	851	1,601	830	1,567
Mineral Fuels and Lubricants	**8,538**	**16,467**	**8,227**	**15,694**	**26,388**	**51,775**	**38,338**	**90,215**
Coal, coke and briquettes	648	86	522	82	1,848	284	2,571	253
Petroleum products and preparations	6,824	15,019	6,705	13,737	21,468	46,850	30,943	84,125
Gas, natural and manufactured	1,025	1,134	975	1,557	2,984	3,893	4,547	4,958
Electric current	41	227	25	317	88	747	276	879
Animal and Vegetables Oils	**259**	**499**	**187**	**377**	**693**	**1,330**	**821**	**1,388**
Animal oils and fats	42	20	36	15	125	50	181	60
Fixed vegetable fats and oils, crude	191	464	128	348	499	1,237	534	1,294
Animal or vegetables fats, processed	26	15	24	14	69	42	106	34
Chemicals and Related Products	**17,249**	**19,079**	**15,858**	**15,922**	**49,219**	**52,078**	**48,863**	**49,085**
Organic chemicals	2,996	3,682	2,726	3,486	8,494	11,364	9,449	13,210
Inorganic chemicals	943	976	852	837	2,586	2,781	2,789	2,951
Dyeing, tanning and coloring materials	659	354	546	282	1,792	937	1,825	950
Medicinial and pharmaceutical products	4,163	8,058	4,391	6,453	12,954	21,136	10,879	17,417
Essential oils and resinoids	1,386	1,155	1,156	1,004	3,684	3,172	3,692	3,052
Fertilizers	328	1,071	282	833	884	2,601	893	2,019
Plastics in primary forms	2,908	1,390	2,491	1,136	8,085	3,776	8,691	3,712
Plastics in nonprimary forms	1,151	877	1,007	699	3,177	2,370	3,044	2,202
Chemical materials and products	2,713	1,515	2,406	1,193	7,563	3,941	7,602	3,572

Part B: NOT Seasonally Adjusted

Exhibit 15. U.S. Trade in Goods by Principal Commodities

In millions of dollars. Details may not equal totals due to rounding. This exhibit is not additive.
(R) - Revised. (X) - Not applicable. (-) Represents zero or less than one-half of measurement shown.

Item (1)	2015						2014	
	March		February		Year-to-Date		Year-to-Date	
	Exports	Imports	Exports	Imports	Exports	Imports	Exports	Imports
Manufactured Goods by Material	**10,052**	**22,821**	**8,954**	**18,428**	**28,067**	**62,883**	**28,597**	**53,290**
Leather and leather manufactures	127	132	103	96	322	335	331	312
Rubber manufactures (4)	854	1,890	731	1,393	2,302	4,942	2,396	5,192
Cork and wood manufactures	189	919	170	699	520	2,395	519	2,063
Paper and paperboard	1,368	1,458	1,213	1,191	3,837	3,934	3,959	3,820
Textile yarn, fabrics	1,151	2,528	1,006	1,983	3,187	6,683	3,219	6,239
Nonmetallic mineral manufactures (4)	1,174	4,079	1,056	3,141	3,244	10,873	3,062	10,332
Iron and steel	1,400	3,788	1,437	3,666	4,294	12,069	4,537	10,358
Nonferrous metals	1,406	3,442	1,167	2,766	3,798	9,675	3,899	3,649
Manufactures of metals	2,382	4,593	2,071	3,494	6,563	11,975	6,676	11,124
Machinery and Transport Equipment	**46,683**	**85,243**	**38,696**	**67,023**	**124,774**	**225,057**	**124,415**	**210,843**
Power generating machinery (4)	3,349	6,193	2,937	4,892	9,471	16,198	9,198	15,357
Specialized industrial machinery	4,287	4,428	3,581	3,272	11,462	11,687	12,220	11,046
Metalworking machinery	510	916	431	637	1,380	2,325	1,309	2,230
General industrial machinery	6,055	9,080	5,214	6,838	16,576	23,377	16,910	22,114
Office machines	1,940	9,897	1,540	7,578	5,232	26,447	5,385	25,812
Telecommunications equipment (4)	1,970	12,708	1,715	9,488	5,653	33,844	5,825	30,649
Electrical machinery (4)	7,125	14,416	5,919	11,463	19,588	38,274	19,382	35,896
Road vehicles	10,380	24,370	8,279	19,439	26,347	63,446	27,662	58,814
Transport equipment (4)	11,067	3,239	9,079	3,417	29,065	9,456	26,524	8,926
Miscellaneous Manufactured Articles	**10,607**	**31,095**	**9,254**	**26,066**	**29,130**	**84,939**	**29,663**	**79,666**
Prefabricated buildings	247	1,067	224	841	686	2,868	732	2,558
Furniture (4)	559	4,130	489	3,129	1,558	10,850	1,463	9,827
Travel goods	54	988	40	763	133	2,636	128	2,436
Apparel and clothing accessories	295	7,677	263	6,804	815	21,699	819	20,899
Footwear	79	2,436	62	2,111	201	6,830	188	6,551
Scientific and controlling equipment (4)	4,472	4,769	3,654	3,928	12,013	12,557	12,270	11,721
Photographic equipment	606	1,237	506	1,118	1,611	3,538	1,535	3,265
Miscellaneous manufactured articles	4,295	8,792	4,015	7,373	12,114	23,961	12,527	22,610
Miscellaneous Commodities	**5,517**	**8,344**	**4,857**	**6,717**	**15,604**	**22,124**	**17,592**	**20,946**
Special transactions	776	6,423	636	4,967	2,018	16,610	1,855	13,835
Coin, including gold coin	15	138	33	99	96	333	107	457
Coin, other than gold	2	2	1	1	6	4	11	4
Gold, nonmonetary	1,954	914	1,450	913	5,297	2,791	6,763	3,823
Low value estimate	2,770	867	2,737	736	8,187	2,386	8,856	3,128
Re-Exports	**18,566**	**(X)**	**17,358**	**(X)**	**53,024**	**(X)**	**52,880**	**(X)**
Manufactured Goods (3)	17,586	(X)	16,361	(X)	50,139	(X)	49,950	(X)
Agricultural Commodities (3)	443	(X)	401	(X)	1,284	(X)	1,329	(X)

(1) Detailed data are presented for domestic exports unless otherwise noted. All data are on a Census basis. The information needed to convert to a BOP basis is not available.

(2) Total exports including re-exports (exports of foreign merchandise).

(3) Manufactured Goods is based on the North American Industry Classification System (NAICS) and Agricultural Commodities is based on the Harmonized System commodities specified by the U.S. Department of Agriculture definition. All other commodity detail is based on the SITC.

(4) Export statistics for certain commodity classifications related to the aircraft industry are subject to suppression and have been aggregated in a manner that prevents the disclosure of confidential information. For additional information, see www.census.gov/foreign-trade/statistics/notices/aircraft/.

NOTE: For information on data sources, nonsampling errors, and definitions, see the information section on page A-1 of this release or at www.census.gov/ft900 or www.bea.gov/newsreleases/international/trade/tradnewsrelease.htm.

Part B: NOT Seasonally Adjusted

Exhibit 16. U.S. Trade in Advanced Technology Products

In millions of dollars. Details may not equal totals due to rounding.

Period	Balance	Exports	Imports
2013			
Jan.- Dec.	-81,287	319,789	401,076
Jan.- Mar.	-16,117	74,652	90,769
January	-7,272	24,010	31,282
February	-5,243	22,660	27,903
March	-3,602	27,982	31,585
April	-7,831	24,691	32,521
May	-6,985	27,141	34,127
June	-3,729	29,198	32,926
July	-7,699	26,735	34,434
August	-5,773	26,734	32,507
September	-8,306	26,751	35,057
October	-9,620	27,696	37,316
November	-9,332	27,949	37,282
December	-5,896	28,242	34,138
2014			
Jan.- Dec.	-85,620	335,909	421,529
Jan.- Mar.	-11,809	78,953	90,762
January	-4,693	25,311	30,004
February	-3,238	24,338	27,576
March	-3,877	29,304	33,181
April	-8,365	26,982	35,348
May	-7,585	27,616	35,200
June	-7,451	28,395	35,845
July	-6,928	27,116	34,045
August	-4,522	28,857	33,378
September	-10,464	28,295	38,760
October	-9,153	30,375	39,528
November	-11,367	28,204	39,571
December	-7,976	31,116	39,092
2015			
Jan.- Mar.	-14,445	82,224	96,669
January	-4,971	27,100	32,071
February	-3,129	25,576	28,705
March	-6,345	29,548	35,892
April			
May			
June			
July			
August			
September			
October			
November			
December			

NOTES:

* Export statistics for certain commodity classifications related to the aircraft industry are subject to suppression and have been aggregated in a manner that prevents the disclosure of confidential information. As a result, Advanced Technology Product exports are overstated by $588 million in March 2015. For additional information, see www.census.gov/foreign-trade/statistics/notices/aircraft/.

* Data are not available on a BOP basis. For information on data sources, nonsampling errors, and definitions, see the information section on page A-1 of this release or at www.census.gov/ft900 or www.bea.gov/newsreleases/international/trade/tradnewsrelease.htm.

Part B: NOT Seasonally Adjusted

Exhibit 16a. U.S. Trade in Advanced Technology Products by Technology Group and Selected Countries and Areas

In millions of dollars. Details may not equal totals due to rounding.

Technology Group	2015 March Balance	March Exports	March Imports	February Balance	February Exports	February Imports	Year-to-Date Balance	Year-to-Date Exports	Year-to-Date Imports	2014 Year-to-Date Balance	Year-to-Date Exports	Year-to-Date Imports
Total	-6,345	29,548	35,892	-3,129	25,576	28,705	-14,445	82,224	96,669	-11,809	78,953	90,762
Advanced Materials	-22	202	224	-25	157	182	-70	533	603	45	545	500
Aerospace (1)	6,909	11,264	4,355	5,119	9,299	4,179	17,802	30,166	12,364	15,343	27,254	11,912
Biotechnology	-337	1,355	1,691	779	1,974	1,196	1,031	5,043	4,013	1,044	3,508	2,464
Electronics	596	3,656	3,060	371	3,046	2,675	1,723	10,361	8,638	1,910	10,359	3,448
Flexible Manufacturing	234	1,567	1,333	298	1,160	862	729	3,954	3,225	895	4,035	3,139
Information and Communications (1)	-11,318	8,041	19,359	-7,953	6,950	14,903	-29,508	22,802	52,310	-24,632	23,162	47,794
Life Science	-1,010	2,823	3,833	-1,148	2,253	3,401	-3,262	7,372	10,634	-2,834	7,789	10,673
Nuclear Technology	2	49	46	103	197	94	54	290	236	-262	293	554
Opto-Electronics (1)	-1,475	444	1,919	-796	354	1,151	-3,238	1,221	4,459	-3,859	1,222	5,081
Weapons	75	147	72	124	186	62	295	482	187	590	787	197

Selected Countries and Areas	2015 March Balance	March Exports	March Imports	February Balance	February Exports	February Imports	Year-to-Date Balance	Year-to-Date Exports	Year-to-Date Imports	2014 Year-to-Date Balance	Year-to-Date Exports	Year-to-Date Imports
Total	-6,345	29,548	35,892	-3,129	25,576	28,705	-14,445	82,224	96,669	-11,809	78,953	90,762
North America	548	5,687	5,139	695	5,128	4,433	1,746	16,061	14,316	2,010	15,455	13,445
Canada	1,208	2,637	1,429	1,274	2,437	1,163	3,446	7,338	3,892	3,393	7,025	3,631
Mexico	-660	3,050	3,710	-579	2,691	3,270	-1,701	8,723	10,424	-1,383	8,431	9,814
European Union	860	7,575	6,715	449	6,632	6,183	1,918	20,697	18,779	309	18,487	18,178
France	72	1,139	1,067	-105	945	1,050	8	3,127	3,119	-771	2,584	3,355
Germany	85	1,444	1,358	-216	1,300	1,516	-279	3,864	4,144	-16	3,831	3,847
Ireland	-1,308	325	1,633	-926	280	1,206	-3,409	793	4,203	-3,294	386	3,981
Italy	25	353	328	-68	236	305	-50	870	920	231	1,048	817
United Kingdom	716	1,356	639	351	1,093	742	1,763	3,759	1,996	1,354	3,524	2,170
Other	1,270	2,959	1,689	1,414	2,778	1,364	3,886	8,284	4,398	2,805	6,314	4,009
Pacific Rim Countries	-10,819	9,666	20,485	-7,150	8,085	15,235	-27,203	27,251	54,453	-23,781	26,580	50,361
Australia	355	459	104	300	372	71	1,147	1,412	265	805	1,061	256
China	-10,002	2,703	12,705	-6,986	2,264	9,250	-26,590	7,586	34,177	-24,120	6,918	31,038
Indonesia	97	177	79	94	150	55	297	491	194	150	336	186
Japan	-887	1,393	2,280	-379	1,256	1,635	-1,493	4,074	5,567	-1,054	4,733	5,787
Malaysia	-1,131	669	1,801	-987	487	1,474	-3,175	1,723	4,898	-2,026	1,653	3,680
Philippines	-116	252	367	-9	242	251	-160	776	936	-106	747	853
Newly Industrialized Countries	770	3,899	3,128	750	3,235	2,485	2,530	10,900	8,369	2,231	10,749	8,518
Hong Kong	1,058	1,097	39	853	892	39	2,799	2,917	118	2,317	2,404	87
Korea, South	-102	1,103	1,205	-245	872	1,118	-513	2,966	3,480	-552	3,081	3,634
Singapore	527	1,019	491	348	709	361	1,352	2,702	1,351	1,408	2,732	1,324
Taiwan	-713	680	1,393	-205	762	968	-1,107	2,313	3,421	-942	2,532	3,474
Other	95	116	21	67	80	13	242	288	46	340	383	43
South/Central America	1,981	2,429	447	1,851	2,329	478	5,543	6,774	1,231	4,347	6,802	2,455
Brazil	436	692	256	402	658	256	1,520	2,157	638	2,373	2,724	351
Other	1,545	1,737	192	1,450	1,671	222	4,023	4,617	594	1,975	4,078	2,104
Other Countries	1,085	4,191	3,105	1,025	3,402	2,377	3,552	11,441	7,889	5,306	11,628	6,322
India	32	208	177	182	309	127	339	790	451	392	850	458
Israel	-1	391	393	-82	227	309	-78	936	1,014	68	840	771
Thailand	-770	251	1,020	-610	214	824	-1,763	955	2,718	-1,185	1,063	2,247
Other	1,825	3,340	1,516	1,535	2,652	1,117	5,054	8,760	3,705	6,031	8,876	2,845

(1) Export statistics for certain commodity classifications related to the aircraft industry are subject to suppression and have been aggregated in a manner that prevents the disclosure of confidential information. As a result, Advanced Technology Product exports are overstated by $588 million in March 2015. For additional information, see www.census.gov/foreign-trade/statistics/notices/aircraft/.

NOTE: Data are not available on a BOP basis. For information on data sources, nonsampling errors, and definitions, see the information section on page A-1 of this release or at www.census.gov/ft900 or www.bea.gov/newsreleases/international/trade/tradnewsrelease.htm.

Part B: NOT Seasonally Adjusted

Exhibit 17. U.S. Imports of Energy-Related Petroleum Products, Including Crude Oil

Details may not equal totals due to rounding.

Period	Total energy-related petroleum products (1)		Crude oil			
	Quantity (thousands of barrels)	Value (thousands of dollars)	Quantity (thousands of barrels)	Thousands of barrels per day (average)	Value (thousands of dollars)	Unit price (dollars)
2014						
Jan.- Dec.	3,381,361	316,635,063	2,700,903	7,400	246,409,332	91.23
Jan.- Mar.	865,795	82,517,010	694,081	7,712	63,727,929	91.82
January	311,606	29,073,951	256,518	8,275	23,141,406	90.21
February	264,514	25,185,466	212,524	7,590	19,452,786	91.53
March	289,676	28,257,593	225,039	7,259	21,133,737	93.91
April	297,175	29,303,921	238,789	7,960	22,799,437	95.48
May	279,613	27,956,136	213,143	6,876	20,487,021	96.12
June	267,192	26,599,392	213,931	7,131	20,625,563	96.41
July	293,953	29,323,258	238,736	7,701	23,351,167	97.81
August	271,322	26,622,325	215,367	6,947	20,744,812	96.32
September	275,988	26,010,134	226,487	7,550	20,960,194	92.54
October	279,141	25,089,810	224,101	7,229	19,826,783	88.47
November	237,927	19,987,564	188,873	6,296	15,667,641	82.95
December	313,254	23,225,512	247,395	7,980	18,218,785	73.64
2015						
Jan.- Mar.	830,163	45,317,378	641,203	7,124	33,165,790	51.72
January	292,867	17,679,621	222,776	7,186	13,133,885	58.96
February	250,650	13,266,616	192,052	6,859	9,511,905	49.53
March	286,647	14,371,141	226,375	7,302	10,520,000	46.47
April						
May						
June						
July						
August						
September						
October						
November						
December						

(1) Details shown for Energy-Related Petroleum Products are not available on a BOP basis. These products include the following SITC commodity groupings: crude oil, petroleum preparations, and liquefied propane and butane gas.

NOTE: For information on data sources, nonsampling errors, and definitions, see the information section on page A-1 of this release or at www.census.gov/ft900 or www.bea.gov/newsreleases/international/trade/tradnewsrelease.htm.

Exhibit 17a. U.S. Imports of Crude Oil by Selected Countries

Details may not equal totals due to rounding. ⊢ Represents zero or less than one-half unit of measurement shown.

Country	Quantity (thousands of barrels)			Customs Value (thousands of dollars)			C.I.F. Value (thousands of dollars)		
	March 2015	February 2015	Year-to-Date 2015	March 2015	February 2015	Year-to-Date 2015	March 2015	February 2015	Year-to-Date 2015
Total	226,375	192,052	641,203	10,520,000	9,511,905	33,165,790	11,070,658	9,967,341	34,689,450
OPEC	76,803	66,669	224,222	3,837,935	3,638,022	12,645,646	4,032,774	3,808,328	3,214,892
Algeria	(-)	(-)	(-)	(-)	(-)	(-)	(-)	⊢)	(-)
Angola	3,261	3,359	8,977	196,697	186,539	544,078	202,592	195,808	563,640
Ecuador	6,360	7,599	23,563	322,033	364,714	1,268,615	340,553	388,277	1,341,926
Iran	(-)	(-)	(-)	(-)	(-)	(-)	(-)	⊢)	(-)
Iraq	5,285	4,934	15,303	283,628	448,296	1,153,253	293,382	457,107	1,183,363
Kuwait	5,455	6,760	21,799	290,218	433,085	1,432,570	300,773	450,125	1,483,194
Libya	197	(-)	483	15,628	(-)	38,377	15,815	⊢)	38,836
Nigeria	1,076	0	2,071	61,252	17	134,546	65,013	7	140,044
Qatar	(-)	(-)	(-)	(-)	(-)	(-)	(-)	⊢)	(-)
Saudi Arabia	29,614	23,876	82,114	1,420,646	1,309,746	4,669,940	1,511,907	1,384,085	4,927,499
United Arab Emirates	602	(-)	602	33,711	(-)	33,711	37,933	⊢)	37,933
Venezuela	24,953	20,139	69,310	1,214,122	895,625	3,370,557	1,264,806	932,907	3,498,458
Non-OPEC	149,573	125,383	416,981	6,682,065	5,873,883	20,520,144	7,037,884	6,159,013	21,474,557
Argentina	1,676	95	2,705	94,411	4,650	149,228	101,241	4,775	161,453
Azerbaijan	(-)	(-)	(-)	(-)	(-)	(-)	(-)	-)	(-)
Bolivia	(-)	(-)	(-)	(-)	(-)	(-)	(-)	-)	(-)
Brazil	4,125	4,529	14,209	212,802	278,717	828,250	223,468	290,357	863,226
Canada	95,435	86,660	276,634	3,902,017	3,783,188	12,874,349	4,158,059	4,003,057	13,587,873
Chad	1,908	2,379	5,710	99,175	129,827	321,460	102,534	131,298	327,798
Colombia	17,615	7,280	36,487	925,060	358,656	1,900,272	962,906	377,121	1,978,284
Congo (Brazzaville)	881	(-)	1,339	53,838	(-)	91,375	54,675	-)	92,647
Congo (Kinshasa)	(-)	(-)	(-)	(-)	(-)	(-)	(-)	-)	(-)
Ecuatorial Guinea	(-)	(-)	(-)	(-)	(-)	(-)	(-)	-)	(-)
Gabon	951	(-)	951	50,000	(-)	50,000	52,406	-)	52,406
Ghana	(-)	(-)	(-)	(-)	(-)	(-)	(-)	-)	(-)
Guatemala	273	238	511	11,750	7,605	19,356	12,335	7,605	19,941
Indonesia	375	857	2,551	21,430	38,890	155,369	22,838	42,222	164,867
Kazakhstan	(-)	(-)	(-)	(-)	(-)	(-)	(-)	-)	(-)
Mexico	25,067	20,699	69,393	1,240,221	1,131,676	3,787,342	1,272,142	1,155,982	3,869,264
Norway	574	592	1,166	31,416	30,870	62,286	33,047	32,403	65,450
Oman	(-)	(-)	(-)	(-)	(-)	(-)	(-)	:-)	(-)
Peru	(-)	(-)	512	(-)	(-)	24,435	(-)	:-)	25,892
Russia	1	700	1,413	145	35,993	72,714	209	37,470	75,732
Thailand	(-)	(-)	(-)	(-)	(-)	(-)	(-)	:-)	(-)
Trinidad and Tobago	(-)	(-)	361	(-)	(-)	20,355	(-)	:-)	21,150
United Kingdom	411	394	1,316	22,695	25,802	77,024	23,861	26,811	79,254
Vietnam	280	195	474	17,093	9,845	26,938	18,152	10,602	28,754
Yemen	(-)	(-)	(-)	(-)	(-)	(-)	(-)	:-)	(-)
Other Non-OPEC	1	765	1,248	12	38,163	59,393	12	39,338	60,568

NOTE: Data are not available on a BOP basis. For information on data sources, nonsampling errors, and definitions, see the information section on page A-1 of this release or at www.census.gov/ft900 or www.bea.gov/newsreleases/international/trade/tradnewsrelease.htm.

Part B: NOT Seasonally Adjusted

Exhibit 18. U.S. Trade in Motor Vehicles and Parts by Selected Countries: 2015

In millions of dollars. Details may not equal totals due to rounding. (X) Not applicable. (-) Represents zero or less than one-half of measurement shown.

Country	Total			Passenger Cars			Trucks, Buses, Special Purpose Vehicles			Parts		
	March	February	Year-to-Date	March	February	Year-to-Date	March	February	Year-to-Date	March	February	Year-to-Date
Exports												
TOTAL	13,836	11,360	36,175	5,070	3,684	12,127	1,752	1,408	4,426	7,014	6,269	19,622
Australia	256	166	643	125	66	319	30	16	60	101	84	265
Belgium	82	75	225	31	18	73	5	5	15	46	51	136
Brazil	168	104	372	47	20	74	22	5	54	99	78	245
Canada	5,194	4,200	13,349	1,465	992	3,221	1,264	1,041	3,159	2,465	2,167	6,969
Chile	80	58	221	26	20	62	23	11	64	32	27	94
China	989	867	2,567	728	654	1,916	5	24	34	256	188	616
Colombia	59	53	148	35	24	66	2	4	8	23	24	75
France	52	54	158	12	9	31	1	2	5	39	43	122
Germany	725	526	1,766	530	355	1,239	9	2	15	186	169	512
Hong Kong	84	49	222	20	16	54	0	(-)	0	64	34	168
Japan	189	160	501	54	28	135	5	7	13	130	125	352
Korea, South	231	160	556	137	81	289	3	2	27	91	77	240
Kuwait	105	96	264	83	72	207	16	20	41	5	4	16
Mexico	2,946	2,719	8,340	231	214	649	111	91	302	2,603	2,414	7,388
Nigeria	47	45	131	31	28	86	11	12	31	6	4	14
Russia	75	76	210	38	46	112	13	6	23	24	24	75
Saudi Arabia	444	244	959	375	199	810	41	19	71	28	26	79
Singapore	29	20	75	1	1	2	1	0	2	27	19	70
South Africa	76	50	211	20	7	51	26	14	73	30	29	87
United Arab Emirates	372	280	962	277	193	687	32	11	57	63	76	218
United Kingdom	289	241	816	155	119	416	6	3	11	128	119	389
Venezuela	42	59	140	18	20	51	6	6	15	18	34	74
Other	1,300	1,059	3,339	632	498	1,576	120	106	345	548	455	1,417
Imports												
TOTAL	31,074	24,903	81,121	14,165	11,605	37,413	3,192	2,482	8,089	13,717	10,816	35,618
Austria	218	176	553	76	56	159	1	1	2	141	120	392
Brazil	90	72	259	0	0	1	6	3	12	84	69	246
Canada	5,199	4,122	13,992	3,456	2,617	9,342	202	169	559	1,541	1,335	4,091
China	1,762	1,263	4,639	16	7	35	32	19	77	1,714	1,237	4,528
Germany	3,447	2,547	8,139	2,387	1,600	5,328	27	12	59	1,033	935	2,752
Italy	545	406	1,171	386	289	781	0	0	1	159	116	389
Japan	4,726	3,682	12,674	3,040	2,695	8,739	58	44	141	1,628	944	3,794
Korea, South	2,116	1,885	6,170	1,294	1,270	4,047	0	0	0	822	615	2,123
Mexico	9,354	8,006	24,558	2,044	1,848	5,357	2,692	2,101	6,792	4,618	4,057	12,409
South Africa	111	49	315	73	21	190	0	(-)	0	37	28	125
Sweden	167	95	361	81	50	162	36	11	82	50	34	117
Taiwan	347	215	787	9	3	15	0	0	1	337	212	771
Thailand	251	188	635	28	36	84	0	1	1	223	151	550
United Kingdom	817	701	2,065	640	563	1,616	53	37	128	124	101	321
Other	1,926	1,495	4,803	634	550	1,559	84	85	234	1,207	860	3,010

NOTE: Data are not available on a BOP basis. For information on data sources, nonsampling errors, and definitions, see the information section on page A-1 of this release or at www.census.gov/ft900 or www.bea.gov/newsreleases/international/trade/tradnewsrelease.htm.

Part C: Seasonally Adjusted (by Geography)

Exhibit 19. U.S. Trade in Goods by Selected Countries and Areas - Census Basis

In millions of dollars. (R) - Revised.

Country and Area	March 2015	February 2015	First Quarter 2014	Second Quarter 2014	Third Quarter 2014	Fourth Quarter 2014	First Quarter 2015	Year-to-Date 2015	Year-to-Date 2014
Balance									
Brazil	406	844	4,530	3,457	2,257	1,787	1,985	1,985	4,580
Canada	-1,436	(R) -1,365	-7,092	-9,513	-9,922	-7,504	-3,803	-3,803	-7,092
China	-37,783	-27,287	-80,034	-85,377	-87,385	-89,836	-94,369	-94,369	-80,034
France	-1,482	-1,570	-4,605	-4,058	-3,510	-3,644	-4,209	-4,209	-4,605
Germany	-5,602	-6,252	-17,343	-19,164	-19,033	-18,199	-18,518	-18,518	-17,343
India	-2,013	-2,002	-5,972	-5,993	-5,830	-5,805	-6,110	-6,110	-5,972
Italy	-2,136	-2,536	-5,673	-6,503	-6,352	-6,566	-7,081	-7,081	-5,673
Japan	-6,333	-4,342	-16,899	-17,209	-16,032	-16,834	-17,222	-17,222	-16,899
Korea, South	-2,569	-2,237	-5,204	-6,015	-5,872	-7,970	-7,866	-7,866	-5,204
Mexico	-4,820	-4,542	-12,275	-12,333	-13,774	-15,450	-13,221	-13,221	-12,275
Saudi Arabia	-63	-445	-11,497	-8,043	-5,334	-3,485	-1,119	-1,119	-11,497
United Kingdom	-177	-507	-1,756	-282	1,663	192	-735	-735	-1,756
All other countries	-7,533	-3,682	-12,700	-11,484	-9,628	-10,784	-14,796	-14,796	-12,700
CAFTA-DR	286	172	426	262	1,063	1,193	891	891	426
European Union	-11,047	-11,001	-32,368	-37,448	-34,585	-36,738	-34,162	-34,162	-32,368
Newly Industrialized Countries	-2,025	509	4,559	1,713	1,883	2,198	-1,913	-1,913	4,559
OPEC	741	340	-20,509	-12,604	-10,288	-6,002	-165	-165	-20,509
South/Central America	2,854	3,634	6,937	8,597	9,640	9,143	8,666	8,666	6,937
Exports									
Brazil	2,700	3,213	11,522	10,710	10,195	9,992	9,157	9,157	11,522
Canada	22,778	(R) 23,332	74,214	78,113	80,699	79,006	70,540	70,540	74,214
China	9,339	8,978	31,791	29,227	29,532	33,474	28,763	28,763	31,791
France	2,332	2,399	7,416	8,116	7,968	7,698	7,476	7,476	7,416
Germany	4,342	4,206	12,951	12,433	12,484	11,575	12,553	12,553	12,951
India	1,844	1,951	5,179	4,929	5,353	6,166	5,534	5,534	5,179
Italy	1,420	1,224	4,345	3,994	4,288	4,361	3,861	3,861	4,345
Japan	5,615	5,393	17,221	16,412	17,127	16,204	16,307	16,307	17,221
Korea, South	3,595	3,397	11,225	11,214	11,147	10,958	10,557	10,557	11,225
Mexico	18,900	19,586	58,646	60,972	60,869	59,839	58,388	58,388	58,646
Saudi Arabia	1,534	1,457	4,176	4,806	4,780	4,916	4,609	4,609	4,176
United Kingdom	4,152	4,269	11,667	13,710	14,787	13,701	13,071	13,071	11,667
All other countries	46,045	46,393	149,440	151,637	151,350	148,815	139,017	139,017	149,440
CAFTA-DR	2,290	2,274	7,831	7,924	7,904	7,672	7,034	7,034	7,831
European Union	22,680	23,499	67,631	70,839	70,816	67,362	69,561	69,561	67,631
Newly Industrialized Countries	10,839	11,211	36,615	35,200	34,844	36,130	33,186	33,186	36,615
OPEC	5,852	6,384	18,802	20,862	21,840	21,226	18,285	18,285	18,802
South/Central America	13,307	13,857	45,826	46,236	47,456	45,277	40,270	40,270	45,826
Imports									
Brazil	2,294	2,368	6,942	7,252	7,938	8,205	7,171	7,171	6,942
Canada	24,215	24,697	81,307	87,625	90,620	86,510	74,343	74,343	81,307
China	47,122	36,265	111,825	114,604	116,917	123,310	123,132	123,132	111,825
France	3,815	3,969	12,021	12,174	11,478	11,342	11,686	11,686	12,021
Germany	9,944	10,458	30,293	31,597	31,517	29,774	31,071	31,071	30,293
India	3,857	3,953	11,151	10,922	11,183	11,972	11,645	11,645	11,151
Italy	3,556	3,760	10,018	10,497	10,640	10,927	10,942	10,942	10,018
Japan	11,949	9,735	34,120	33,622	33,159	33,038	33,528	33,528	34,120
Korea, South	6,164	5,634	16,429	17,229	17,019	18,928	18,424	18,424	16,429
Mexico	23,721	24,129	70,921	73,304	74,643	75,290	71,609	71,609	70,921
Saudi Arabia	1,596	1,902	15,673	12,849	10,115	8,401	5,728	5,728	15,673
United Kingdom	4,330	4,777	13,423	13,993	13,124	13,509	13,806	13,806	13,423
All other countries	53,578	50,075	162,140	163,121	160,978	159,599	153,813	153,813	162,140
CAFTA-DR	2,004	2,103	7,405	7,662	6,841	6,479	6,143	6,143	7,405
European Union	33,727	34,500	100,049	108,286	105,402	104,100	103,723	103,723	100,049
Newly Industrialized Countries	12,864	10,702	32,056	33,487	32,961	33,931	35,099	35,099	32,056
OPEC	5,112	6,044	39,311	33,466	32,127	27,227	18,450	18,450	39,311
South/Central America	10,453	10,224	38,841	37,639	37,816	36,134	31,604	31,604	38,841

NOTES:

* Countries may be included in more than one area. For a list of countries in each area, see the information section on page A-1 of this release or at www.census.gov/ft900 or www.bea.gov/newsreleases/international/trade/tradnewsrelease.htm.
* Area data reflect the composition of the areas as they were as of the most recent statistical period.
* Seasonally adjusted country and area data in this exhibit will not sum to the commodity-based seasonally adjusted totals shown in Part A of this release. Data users should use caution drawing comparisons between the two sets of seasonally adjusted series.
* For information on data sources, nonsampling errors, and definitions, see the information section on page A-1 of this release or at www.census.gov/ft900 or www.bea.gov/newsreleases/international/trade/tradnewsrelease.htm.

Part C: Seasonally Adjusted (by Geography)

Exhibit 20. U.S. Trade in Goods and Services by Selected Countries and Areas - BOP Basis

In millions of dollars.

Country and Area	Third Quarter 2013	Fourth Quarter 2013	First Quarter 2014	Second Quarter 2014	Third Quarter 2014	Fourth Quarter 2014	Annual 2012	Annual 2013	Annual 2014
Balance									
Brazil	9,079	8,762	9,763	8,293	7,457	6,594	29,252	36,145	32,107
Canada	-1,676	19	-416	-2,575	-3,147	-959	-5,071	-2,508	-7,096
China	-74,498	-73,583	-73,673	-78,277	-80,676	-83,414	-295,293	-295,344	-316,041
France	-2,534	-2,478	-3,180	-2,929	-2,981	-3,390	-9,770	-10,255	-12,480
Germany	-19,220	-18,173	-18,672	-20,876	-20,103	-18,982	-65,441	-72,944	-78,633
India	-6,524	-6,507	-7,180	-7,356	-7,223	-6,728	-24,542	-25,360	-28,488
Italy	-5,532	-6,478	-6,195	-6,924	-7,097	-7,347	-23,247	-23,669	-27,563
Japan	-14,841	-13,492	-13,097	-14,022	-12,390	-12,887	-58,369	-58,491	-52,396
Korea, South	-1,947	-1,015	-2,284	-2,666	-3,221	-5,134	-7,689	-9,323	-13,304
Mexico	-12,488	-11,979	-11,387	-11,777	-13,180	-14,956	-53,993	-47,848	-51,300
Saudi Arabia	-6,999	-7,678	-9,403	-6,567	-3,528	-2,091	-30,911	-25,243	-21,588
United Kingdom	1,658	1,364	1,090	2,969	5,258	3,682	11,357	7,041	13,000
All other countries	16,321	15,145	10,637	15,817	17,061	15,556	-3,886	51,406	59,071
CAFTA-DR	n.a.	n.a.	n.a.	n.a.	n.a.	n.a.	n.a.	n.a.	n.a.
European Union	-19,986	-23,877	-23,058	-25,005	-20,890	-22,824	-76,259	-84,542	-91,777
Newly Industrialized Countries	10,916	12,085	10,997	9,610	8,892	8,833	33,387	40,969	38,332
OPEC	-12,736	-12,269	-15,005	-7,586	-5,161	-1,818	-82,756	-49,419	-29,570
South/Central America	14,858	14,473	13,326	15,695	15,607	15,162	30,994	53,928	59,790
Exports									
Brazil	18,194	17,265	18,351	17,672	17,317	16,908	68,623	70,712	70,248
Canada	91,349	93,559	90,205	94,090	96,882	94,893	355,623	366,329	376,072
China	39,494	44,976	42,094	40,447	40,297	43,778	144,879	160,599	166,617
France	13,200	13,471	12,735	13,494	12,776	12,424	49,115	51,577	51,430
Germany	18,568	19,246	20,120	19,491	19,645	18,788	76,270	75,251	78,045
India	8,709	8,786	8,745	8,635	9,209	10,654	34,626	35,695	37,243
Italy	7,023	6,505	6,821	6,457	6,250	6,405	24,947	26,248	25,932
Japan	28,163	28,337	29,206	28,344	29,078	28,540	118,009	112,782	115,167
Korea, South	16,363	17,171	16,836	17,119	16,433	16,491	62,322	64,408	66,881
Mexico	64,316	65,295	66,114	68,494	68,482	67,333	244,631	256,615	270,424
Saudi Arabia	6,995	6,853	6,623	6,650	6,957	6,635	25,935	28,011	26,865
United Kingdom	27,071	27,036	27,182	29,574	30,812	30,184	115,186	108,669	117,752
All other countries	231,327	230,196	232,221	238,242	236,365	235,024	896,374	923,299	941,853
CAFTA-DR	n.a.	n.a.	n.a.	n.a.	n.a.	n.a.	n.a.	n.a.	n.a.
European Union	119,319	118,367	121,350	126,468	126,757	124,443	468,846	471,566	499,019
Newly Industrialized Countries	49,791	50,188	50,937	51,007	49,832	51,059	188,781	196,801	202,834
OPEC	27,765	27,368	26,854	28,685	29,288	28,365	109,328	114,169	113,192
South/Central America	73,395	71,608	70,858	72,491	71,885	69,995	278,210	286,702	285,229
Imports									
Brazil	9,115	8,502	8,588	9,378	9,860	10,314	39,370	34,567	38,141
Canada	93,025	93,540	90,622	96,665	100,029	95,852	360,694	368,836	383,168
China	113,992	118,559	115,767	118,724	120,973	127,193	440,172	455,943	482,658
France	15,734	15,948	15,916	16,423	15,757	15,814	58,885	61,832	63,910
Germany	37,788	37,419	38,792	40,367	39,749	37,770	141,711	148,195	156,677
India	15,234	15,293	15,926	15,991	16,432	17,382	59,168	61,054	65,731
Italy	12,555	12,983	13,016	13,381	13,347	13,752	48,194	49,917	53,495
Japan	43,004	41,829	42,303	42,365	41,468	41,427	176,378	171,273	167,563
Korea, South	18,310	18,186	19,120	19,785	19,654	21,625	70,012	73,731	80,184
Mexico	76,804	77,273	77,501	80,271	81,662	82,290	298,625	304,463	321,724
Saudi Arabia	13,994	14,531	16,026	13,217	10,485	8,726	56,846	53,254	48,453
United Kingdom	25,413	25,672	26,092	26,604	25,554	26,503	103,829	101,627	104,752
All other countries	215,006	215,051	221,584	222,426	219,304	219,468	900,261	871,893	882,782
CAFTA-DR	n.a.	n.a.	n.a.	n.a.	n.a.	n.a.	n.a.	n.a.	n.a.
European Union	139,305	142,244	144,408	151,473	147,647	147,267	545,105	556,108	590,796
Newly Industrialized Countries	38,876	38,103	39,939	41,396	40,940	42,226	155,394	155,832	164,502
OPEC	40,502	39,637	41,859	36,272	34,449	30,183	192,084	163,588	142,763
South/Central America	58,536	57,135	57,531	56,796	56,277	54,833	247,216	232,775	225,439

n.a. Not available

NOTES:

* Countries may be included in more than one area. For a list of countries in each area and for additional information on country and area detail for goods on a BOP basis and for services, see the information section on page A-1 of this release or at www.census.gov/ft900 or www.bea.gov/newsreleases/international/trade/tradnewsrelease.htm.

* Area data reflect the composition of the areas as they were at the time of reporting.

* Seasonally adjusted country and area data in this exhibit will not sum to the seasonally adjusted totals shown in Part A of this release. Data users should use caution drawing comparisons between the two sets of seasonally adjusted series.

* For information on data sources, nonsampling errors, and definitions, see the information section that begins on page A-1 of this release or at www.census.gov/ft900 or www.bea.gov/newsreleases/international/trade/tradnewsrelease.htm.

* Statistics for the first quarter 2015 will be available with the April 2015 release on June 3, 2015.

Part C: Seasonally Adjusted (by Geography)

Exhibit 20a. U.S. Trade in Goods by Selected Countries and Areas - BOP Basis

In millions of dollars.

Country and Area	Third Quarter 2013	Fourth Quarter 2013	First Quarter 2014	Second Quarter 2014	Third Quarter 2014	Fourth Quarter 2014	Annual 2012	Annual 2013	Annual 2014
Balance									
Brazil	4,235	3,954	4,651	3,578	2,625	1,996	11,757	16,852	12,850
Canada	-9,697	-8,360	-8,469	-10,777	-11,215	-9,003	-35,804	-35,336	-39,433
China	-80,761	-30,022	-80,240	-85,291	-87,081	-90,264	-315,010	-318,778	-342,875
France	-3,506	-3,633	-4,565	-4,114	-3,556	-3,754	-11,138	-14,524	-15,939
Germany	-17,612	-17,273	-17,573	-19,392	-19,144	-18,280	-61,076	-67,600	-74,339
India	-5,092	-5,100	-5,915	-5,959	-5,822	-5,167	-18,397	-19,789	-22,833
Italy	-5,337	-6,040	-5,725	-6,546	-6,389	-6,619	-21,093	-22,196	-25,278
Japan	-18,929	-17,385	-17,310	-17,783	-16,338	-17,014	-77,690	-74,755	-68,446
Korea, South	-5,077	-3,589	-4,889	-5,582	-5,528	-7,676	-15,250	-19,471	-23,675
Mexico	-15,544	-14,754	-14,042	-13,998	-15,559	-17,177	-66,729	-59,937	-60,776
Saudi Arabia	-9,171	-9,564	-11,624	-8,080	-5,727	-3,842	-37,767	-33,121	-29,273
United Kingdom	-1,477	-1,487	-1,953	-251	1,556	136	-319	-5,448	-512
All other countries	-8,998	-8,626	-13,544	-11,031	-9,718	-10,805	-93,578	-47,565	-45,098
CAFTA-DR	55	2	365	190	958	1,114	-1,367	-817	2,627
European Union	-30,162	-34,027	-33,774	-37,692	-34,337	-36,532	-118,006	-126,916	-142,336
Newly Industrialized Countries	4,510	6,636	5,249	2,431	2,396	2,474	14,225	18,493	12,550
OPEC	-18,321	-17,878	-21,032	-12,689	-10,726	-6,805	-101,598	-70,827	-51,252
South/Central America	7,881	7,226	6,876	8,601	9,782	9,288	10,865	25,677	34,547
Exports									
Brazil	11,560	10,574	11,515	10,702	10,202	9,982	43,577	44,072	42,401
Canada	75,700	77,617	74,522	78,435	81,067	79,101	294,090	303,048	313,125
China	29,679	35,057	31,954	29,730	30,257	33,135	111,789	122,838	125,076
France	8,447	8,594	7,516	8,214	8,080	7,758	31,257	32,089	31,537
Germany	11,900	11,975	13,012	12,508	12,582	11,616	49,266	47,722	49,717
India	5,319	5,327	5,266	5,021	5,417	6,837	22,276	22,225	22,542
Italy	4,485	4,211	4,399	4,038	4,324	4,377	16,231	16,896	17,139
Japan	16,636	16,781	17,450	16,691	17,431	16,564	71,480	66,512	68,137
Korea, South	10,562	11,897	11,623	11,708	11,595	11,227	44,337	43,504	46,154
Mexico	56,727	57,849	58,708	61,089	61,006	59,963	216,426	226,760	240,736
Saudi Arabia	4,399	4,624	4,064	4,790	4,416	4,572	17,989	18,770	17,842
United Kingdom	11,932	11,922	11,878	13,914	14,965	13,836	56,012	48,400	54,593
All other countries	150,400	149,038	150,462	153,431	152,402	149,779	586,959	599,947	606,073
CAFTA-DR	7,665	7,599	7,847	7,931	7,886	7,664	29,884	29,654	31,328
European Union	68,219	36,782	68,502	71,648	71,654	67,901	269,397	265,654	279,705
Newly Industrialized Countries	35,797	36,893	37,530	36,223	35,630	36,427	139,296	143,588	145,809
OPEC	19,727	19,352	18,513	21,100	21,231	20,878	80,765	83,093	81,721
South/Central America	47,856	45,747	45,985	46,412	47,567	45,449	183,704	185,094	185,412
Imports									
Brazil	7,325	6,620	6,864	7,124	7,577	7,986	31,820	27,221	29,551
Canada	85,397	85,977	82,991	89,212	92,282	88,103	329,894	338,384	352,539
China	110,440	115,079	112,194	115,021	117,337	123,399	426,799	441,616	467,951
France	11,953	12,226	12,081	12,328	11,636	11,512	42,395	46,613	47,557
Germany	29,511	29,248	30,584	31,900	31,726	29,895	110,342	115,323	124,106
India	10,411	10,428	11,181	10,981	11,239	12,004	40,673	42,014	45,405
Italy	9,822	10,251	10,124	10,584	10,713	10,996	37,324	39,092	42,417
Japan	35,565	34,165	34,761	34,475	33,769	33,578	149,170	141,267	136,583
Korea, South	15,639	15,486	16,512	17,290	17,123	18,903	59,587	62,975	69,829
Mexico	72,271	72,603	72,751	75,086	76,564	77,140	283,155	286,697	301,541
Saudi Arabia	13,570	14,187	15,688	12,870	10,143	8,415	55,756	51,891	47,116
United Kingdom	13,409	13,410	13,831	14,165	13,409	13,700	56,332	53,849	55,105
All other countries	159,398	157,664	164,006	164,462	162,120	160,584	680,537	647,512	651,171
CAFTA-DR	7,611	7,597	7,482	7,741	6,928	6,551	31,251	30,471	28,702
European Union	98,382	100,809	102,276	109,340	105,991	104,433	387,403	392,570	422,041
Newly Industrialized Countries	31,288	30,258	32,281	33,791	33,234	33,953	125,072	125,095	133,250
OPEC	38,049	37,229	39,545	33,789	31,957	27,683	182,364	153,920	132,974
South/Central America	39,975	38,521	39,109	37,811	37,785	36,160	172,839	159,417	150,865

NOTES:

* Countries may be included in more than one area. For a list of countries in each area and for additional information on country and area detail for goods on a BOP basis and for services, see the information section on page A-1 of this release or at www.census.gov/ft900 or www.bea.gov/newsreleases/international/trade/tradnewsrelease.htm.
* Area data reflect the composition of the areas as they were at the time of reporting.
* Seasonally adjusted country and area data in this exhibit will not sum to the seasonally adjusted totals shown in Part A of this release. Data users should use caution drawing comparisons between the two sets of seasonally adjusted series.
* For information on data sources, nonsampling errors, and definitions, see the information section that begins on page A-1 of this release or at www.census.gov/ft900 or www.bea.gov/newsreleases/international/trade/tradnewsrelease.htm.
* Statistics for the first quarter 2015 will be available with the April 2015 release on June 3, 2015.

Part C: Seasonally Adjusted (by Geography)

Exhibit 20b. U.S. Trade in Services by Selected Countries and Areas

In millions of dollars.

Country and Area	Third Quarter 2013	Fourth Quarter 2013	First Quarter 2014	Second Quarter 2014	Third Quarter 2014	Fourth Quarter 2014	Annual 2012	Annual 2013	Annual 2014
Balance									
Brazil	4,844	4,809	5,112	4,715	4,832	4,598	17,496	19,293	19,257
Canada	8,021	8,379	8,052	8,202	8,069	8,044	30,733	32,829	32,367
China	6,263	6,439	6,567	7,013	6,405	6,849	19,717	23,434	26,834
France	972	1,155	1,384	1,185	575	364	1,368	4,269	3,509
Germany	-1,608	-900	-1,099	-1,483	-959	-702	-4,366	-5,344	-4,244
India	-1,433	-1,407	-1,265	-1,397	-1,401	-1,561	-6,145	-5,571	-5,625
Italy	-195	-439	-470	-378	-708	-728	-2,155	-1,473	-2,285
Japan	4,089	3,892	4,213	3,762	3,948	4,127	19,321	16,264	16,050
Korea, South	3,130	2,574	2,605	2,916	2,307	2,543	7,561	10,148	10,371
Mexico	3,056	2,776	2,655	2,221	2,379	2,221	12,736	12,089	9,476
Saudi Arabia	2,172	1,886	2,221	1,513	2,199	1,752	6,857	7,878	7,685
United Kingdom	3,136	2,851	3,043	3,221	3,702	3,545	11,676	12,490	13,511
All other countries	25,319	23,770	24,181	26,847	26,779	26,361	89,692	98,971	104,169
CAFTA-DR	n.a.	n.a.	n.a.	n.a.	n.a.	n.a.	n.a.	n.a.	n.a.
European Union	10,176	10,151	10,716	12,687	13,448	13,708	41,747	42,374	50,559
Newly Industrialized Countries	6,406	5,449	5,749	7,179	6,496	6,359	19,163	22,476	25,783
OPEC	5,585	5,609	6,028	5,103	5,564	4,987	18,842	21,408	21,682
South/Central America	6,977	7,247	6,451	7,094	5,825	5,873	20,129	28,251	25,243
Exports									
Brazil	6,634	6,691	6,835	6,970	7,115	6,926	25,046	26,640	27,847
Canada	15,649	15,942	15,683	15,655	15,815	15,793	61,533	63,281	62,946
China	9,815	9,919	10,140	10,717	10,041	10,643	33,090	37,761	41,541
France	4,753	4,877	5,220	5,280	4,696	4,666	17,858	19,488	19,862
Germany	6,669	7,271	7,109	6,984	7,064	7,172	27,004	27,529	28,328
India	3,390	3,459	3,479	3,613	3,792	3,818	12,350	13,470	14,702
Italy	2,538	2,294	2,421	2,418	1,926	2,028	8,716	9,352	8,793
Japan	11,527	11,556	11,756	11,652	11,647	11,975	46,529	46,270	47,031
Korea, South	5,801	5,275	5,213	5,411	4,838	5,264	17,986	20,904	20,727
Mexico	7,589	7,446	7,406	7,406	7,476	7,370	28,205	29,855	29,658
Saudi Arabia	2,596	2,229	2,559	1,860	2,541	2,063	7,947	9,240	9,023
United Kingdom	15,140	15,114	15,304	15,660	15,847	16,348	59,173	60,269	63,159
All other countries	80,928	81,158	81,759	84,811	83,964	85,245	309,415	323,352	335,780
CAFTA-DR	n.a.	n.a.	n.a.	n.a.	n.a.	n.a.	n.a.	n.a.	n.a.
European Union	51,099	51,585	52,849	54,820	55,103	56,542	199,449	205,912	219,314
Newly Industrialized Countries	13,994	13,294	13,407	14,784	14,202	14,632	49,485	53,213	57,025
OPEC	8,038	8,016	8,341	7,585	8,057	7,488	28,562	31,076	31,471
South/Central America	25,538	25,861	24,873	26,080	24,318	24,546	94,506	101,608	99,817
Imports									
Brazil	1,790	1,882	1,724	2,255	2,283	2,328	7,550	7,347	8,590
Canada	7,628	7,563	7,631	7,453	7,747	7,748	30,799	30,452	30,579
China	3,551	3,480	3,573	3,704	3,636	3,794	13,373	14,327	14,707
France	3,781	3,722	3,835	4,095	4,121	4,302	16,490	15,219	16,353
Germany	8,277	8,172	8,207	8,467	8,023	7,874	31,369	32,873	32,572
India	4,823	4,865	4,745	5,010	5,193	5,379	18,495	19,041	20,327
Italy	2,733	2,732	2,891	2,797	2,634	2,756	10,871	10,825	11,078
Japan	7,439	7,664	7,543	7,891	7,699	7,849	27,208	30,006	30,981
Korea, South	2,671	2,701	2,608	2,495	2,531	2,722	10,424	10,756	10,355
Mexico	4,533	4,670	4,750	5,185	5,097	5,149	15,469	17,766	20,182
Saudi Arabia	423	343	338	347	342	311	1,090	1,362	1,338
United Kingdom	12,004	12,262	12,261	12,439	12,144	12,803	47,497	47,779	49,647
All other countries	55,609	57,388	57,578	57,964	57,185	58,884	219,723	224,381	231,611
CAFTA-DR	n.a.	n.a.	n.a.	n.a.	n.a.	n.a.	n.a.	n.a.	n.a.
European Union	40,923	41,434	42,132	42,133	41,655	42,834	157,702	163,538	168,755
Newly Industrialized Countries	7,588	7,845	7,658	7,605	7,706	8,273	30,322	30,737	31,242
OPEC	2,453	2,407	2,314	2,482	2,493	2,500	9,720	9,668	9,789
South/Central America	18,561	18,614	18,422	18,986	18,493	18,673	74,377	73,357	74,574

n.a. Not available

NOTES:
* Countries may be included in more than one area. For a list of countries in each area and for additional information on country and area detail for goods on a BOP basis and for services, see the information section on page A-1 of this release or at www.census.gov/ft900 or www.bea.gov/newsreleases/international/trade/tradnewsrelease.htm.
* Area data reflect the composition of the areas as they were at the time of reporting.
* Seasonally adjusted country and area data in this exhibit will not sum to the seasonally adjusted totals shown in Part A of this release. Data users should use caution drawing comparisons between the two sets of seasonally adjusted series.
* For information on data sources, nonsampling errors, and definitions, see the information section that begins on page A-1 of this release or at www.census.gov/ft900 or www.bea.gov/newsreleases/international/trade/tradnewsrelease.htm.
* Statistics for the first quarter 2015 will be available with the April 2015 release on June 3, 2015.

INFORMATION ON GOODS AND SERVICES

GOODS (CENSUS BASIS)

Data for goods on a Census basis are compiled from the documents collected by the U.S. Customs and Border Protection and reflect the movement of goods between foreign countries and the 50 states, the District of Columbia, Puerto Rico, the U.S. Virgin Islands, and U.S. Foreign Trade Zones. They include government and non-government shipments of goods and exclude shipments between the United States and its territories and possessions; transactions with U.S. military, diplomatic, and consular installations abroad; U.S. goods returned to the United States by its Armed Forces; personal and household effects of travelers; and in-transit shipments. The General Imports value reflects the total arrival of merchandise from foreign countries that immediately enters consumption channels, warehouses, or Foreign Trade Zones.

For imports, the value reported is the U.S. Customs and Border Protection appraised value of merchandise—generally, the price paid for merchandise for export to the United States. Import duties, freight, insurance, and other charges incurred in bringing merchandise to the United States are excluded. The exception is Exhibit 17a, which shows CIF import value. The CIF (cost, insurance, and freight) value represents the landed value of the merchandise at the first port of arrival in the United States. It is computed by adding import charges to the customs value and therefore excludes U.S. import duties.

Exports are valued at the f.a.s. (free alongside ship) value of merchandise at the U.S. port of export, based on the transaction price including inland freight, insurance, and other charges incurred in placing the merchandise alongside the carrier at the U.S. port of exportation.

REVISION PROCEDURE (CENSUS BASIS)

Monthly Revisions: Monthly data include actual month's transactions as well as a small number of transactions for previous months. Each month, the U.S. Census Bureau revises the aggregate seasonally adjusted (current and real chained-dollar) and unadjusted export, import, and trade balance figures, as well as the end-use totals for the prior month. Country detail data and commodity detail data, based on the Standard International Trade Classification (SITC) Revision 4 and the North American Industry Classification System (NAICS), are not revised monthly. The timing adjustment shown in Exhibit 14 is the difference between monthly data as originally reported and as recompiled.

For February, unadjusted exports of goods were revised downward less than $0.1 billion and unadjusted imports of goods were revised upward $0.4 billion. Goods carry-over in March was $0.1 billion (0.1 percent) for exports and $2.3 billion (1.2 percent) for imports. For February, revised export carry-over was less than $0.1 billion (less than 0.1 percent) and revised import carry-over was $0.1 billion (0.1 percent).

Quarterly Revisions to Chain-Weighted Dollar Series: For March, June, September, and December statistical month releases, revisions are made to the real chained-dollar series presented in Exhibits 10 and 11: the previous five months are revised to incorporate the Bureau of Labor Statistics' revisions to price indexes, which are used to produce the real chained-dollar series and to align Census data with data published by the U.S. Bureau of Economic Analysis (BEA) in the National Income and Product Accounts (NIPAs).

Annual Revisions: Each June, not seasonally adjusted goods data are revised to redistribute monthly data that arrived too late for inclusion in the month of transaction. In addition, revisions are made to reflect corrections received subsequent to the monthly revisions. Seasonally adjusted data are also revised to reflect recalculated seasonal and trading-day adjustments. These revisions are reflected in totals, end-use, commodity, and country summary data.

Other Revisions: For December and January statistical month releases, each prior month of the most recent full year is revised so that the totals of the seasonally adjusted months equal the annual totals.

U.S./CANADA DATA EXCHANGE AND SUBSTITUTION

Data for U.S. exports to Canada are derived from import data compiled by Canada. The use of Canada's import data to produce U.S. export data requires several alignments in order to compare the two series.

1. *Coverage* - Canadian imports are based on country of origin. U.S. goods shipped from a third country are included. U.S. exports exclude these foreign shipments. For March 2015, these shipments totaled $191.8 million. U.S. export coverage also excludes U.S. postal shipments to Canada. For March 2015, these shipments totaled $20.0 million.

   U.S. import coverage includes shipments of railcars and locomotives from Canada. Effective with January 2004 statistics, Canada excludes these shipments from its goods exports to the United States, therefore creating coverage differences between the two countries for these goods.

2. *Valuation* - Canadian imports are valued at the point of origin in the United States. However, U.S. exports are valued at the port of exit in the United States and include inland freight charges, making the U.S. export value slightly larger than the Canadian import value. Canada requires inland freight to be reported separately from the value of the goods. Combining the inland freight and the Canadian reported import value provides a consistent valuation for all U.S. exports. Inland freight charges for March 2015 accounted for 2.0 percent of the value of U.S. exports to Canada.

3. *Re-exports* - Unlike Canadian imports, which are based on country of origin, U.S. exports include re-exports of foreign goods. Therefore, the aggregate U.S. export figure is slightly larger than the Canadian import figure. For March 2015, re-exports to Canada were $4,271.6 million.

4. *Exchange Rate* - Average monthly exchange rates are applied to convert the published data to U.S. currency. For March 2015, the average exchange rate was 1.2618 Canadian dollars per U.S. dollar.

5. *Other* - There are other minor differences, such as rounding error, that are statistically insignificant.

Canadian Estimates: Effective with January 2001 statistics, the current month data for exports to Canada contain an estimate for late arrivals and corrections. The following month, this estimate is replaced, in the news release exhibits only, with the actual value of late receipts and corrections. This estimate improves the current month data for exports to Canada and treats late receipts for exports to Canada in a manner that is more consistent with the treatment of late receipts for exports to other countries.

NONSAMPLING ERRORS

The goods data are a complete enumeration of documents collected by the U.S. Customs and Border Protection and are not subject to sampling errors. Quality assurance procedures are performed at every stage of collection, processing, and tabulation. However, the data are still subject to several types of nonsampling errors. The most significant of these include reporting errors, undocumented shipments, timeliness, data capture errors, and errors in the estimation of low-valued transactions.

Reporting Errors: Reporting errors are mistakes or omissions made by importers, exporters, or their agents in their import or export declarations. Most errors involve missing or invalid commodity classification codes and missing or incorrect quantities or shipping weights. They have a negligible effect on aggregate import, export, and balance of trade statistics. However, they can affect the detailed commodity statistics.

Undocumented Shipments: Federal regulations require importers, exporters, or their agents to report all merchandise shipments above established exemption levels. The U.S. Census Bureau has determined that not all required documents are filed, particularly for exports.

Timeliness and Data Capture Errors: The U.S. Census Bureau captures import and export information from administrative documents and through various automated collection programs. Documents may be lost, and data may be incorrectly keyed, coded, or recorded. Transactions may be included in a subsequent month's statistics if received late.

Low-valued Transactions: The total values of transactions valued as much as or below $2,500 for exports and $2,000 ($250 for certain quota items) for imports are estimated for each country, using factors based on the ratios of low-valued shipments to individual country totals for past periods.

The U.S. Census Bureau recommends that data users incorporate this information into their analyses, as nonsampling errors could impact the conclusion drawn from the results. For a detailed discussion of errors affecting the goods data, see "U.S. Merchandise Trade Statistics: A Quality Profile," available at www.census.gov/foreign-trade/aip/quality_profile10032014.pdf or from the Economic Indicators Division, U.S. Census Bureau.

AREA GROUPINGS

North America: Canada, Mexico.

Dominican Republic-Central America-United States Free Trade Agreement (CAFTA-DR): Costa Rica, Dominican Republic, El Salvador, Guatemala, Honduras, Nicaragua.

Europe: Albania, Andorra, Armenia, Austria, Azerbaijan, Belarus, Belgium, Bosnia and Herzegovina, Bulgaria, Croatia, Cyprus, Czech Republic, Denmark, Estonia, Faroe Islands, Finland, France, Georgia, Germany, Gibraltar, Greece, Hungary, Iceland, Ireland, Italy, Kazakhstan, Kosovo, Kyrgyzstan, Latvia, Liechtenstein, Lithuania, Luxembourg, Macedonia, Malta, Moldova, Monaco, Montenegro, Netherlands, Norway, Poland, Portugal, Romania, Russia, San Marino, Serbia, Slovakia, Slovenia, Spain, Svalbard-Jan Mayen Island, Sweden, Switzerland, Tajikistan, Turkey, Turkmenistan, Ukraine, United Kingdom, Uzbekistan, Vatican City.

European Union: Austria, Belgium, Bulgaria, Croatia, Cyprus, Czech Republic, Denmark, Estonia, Finland, France, Germany, Greece, Hungary, Ireland, Italy, Latvia, Lithuania, Luxembourg, Malta, Netherlands, Poland, Portugal, Romania, Slovakia, Slovenia, Spain, Sweden, United Kingdom.

Euro Area: Austria, Belgium, Cyprus, Estonia, Finland, France, Germany, Greece, Ireland, Italy, Latvia, Lithuania, Luxembourg, Malta, Netherlands, Portugal, Slovakia, Slovenia, Spain.

Newly Industrialized Countries (NICs): Hong Kong, Korea (South), Singapore, Taiwan.

Pacific Rim: Australia, Brunei, China, Hong Kong, Indonesia, Japan, Korea (South), Macau, Malaysia, New Zealand, Papua New Guinea, Philippines, Singapore, Taiwan.

South/Central America: Anguilla, Antigua and Barbuda, Argentina, Aruba, Bahamas, Barbados, Belize, Bermuda, Bolivia, Brazil, British Virgin Islands, Cayman Islands, Chile, Colombia, Costa Rica, Cuba, Curacao, Dominica, Dominican Republic, Ecuador, El Salvador, Falkland Islands (Islas Malvinas), French Guiana, Grenada, Guadeloupe, Guatemala, Guyana, Haiti, Honduras, Jamaica, Martinique, Montserrat, Netherlands Antilles, Nicaragua, Panama, Paraguay, Peru, Sint Maarten, St. Kitts and Nevis, St. Lucia, St. Vincent and the Grenadines, Suriname, Trinidad and Tobago, Turks and Caicos Islands, Uruguay, Venezuela.

OPEC: Algeria, Angola, Ecuador, Iran, Iraq, Kuwait, Libya, Nigeria, Qatar, Saudi Arabia, United Arab Emirates, Venezuela.

Africa: Algeria, Angola, Benin, Botswana, British Indian Ocean Territories, Burkina Faso, Burundi, Cabo Verde, Cameroon, Central African Republic, Chad, Comoros, Congo (Brazzaville), Congo (Kinshasa), Djibouti, Egypt, Equatorial Guinea, Eritrea, Ethiopia, French Southern and Antarctic Lands, Gabon, Gambia, Ghana, Guinea, Guinea-Bissau, Ivory Coast, Kenya, Lesotho, Liberia, Libya, Madagascar, Malawi, Mali, Mauritania, Mauritius, Mayotte, Morocco, Mozambique, Namibia, Niger, Nigeria, Reunion, Rwanda, St. Helena, Sao Tome and Principe, Senegal, Seychelles, Sierra Leone, Somalia, South Africa, South Sudan, Sudan, Swaziland, Tanzania, Togo, Tunisia, Uganda, Western Sahara, Zambia, Zimbabwe.

ADJUSTMENTS FOR SEASONAL AND TRADING-DAY VARIATIONS

Goods are initially classified under the Harmonized Commodity Description and Coding System (Harmonized System), which is an internationally accepted standard for the commodity classification of traded goods. The Harmonized System describes and measures the characteristics of the goods and is the basis for the systems used in the United States: Schedule B for exports and Harmonized Tariff Schedule for imports. Combining trade into approximately 140 export and 140 import end-use categories makes it possible to examine goods according to their principal uses (see Exhibits 7 and 8). These categories are used as the basis for computing the seasonal and trading-day adjusted data. These adjusted data are then summed to the six end-use aggregates for publication (see Exhibit 6). These data are provided to BEA, from the U.S. Census Bureau, for use in the NIPAs and in the U.S International Transactions Accounts (balance of payments accounts).

Exhibit 19 shows goods (Census Basis) that are seasonally adjusted for selected countries and world areas. Unlike the commodity-based adjustments discussed above, these adjustments are developed and applied directly at the country and world area levels. For total exports and imports, data users should refer to the commodity-based totals shown in the other exhibits. The seasonally adjusted country and world area data will not sum to the seasonally adjusted commodity-based totals because the seasonally adjusted country and world area data and the commodity-based totals are derived from different aggregations of the export and import data and from different seasonal adjustment models. Data users should use caution drawing comparisons between the two sets of seasonally adjusted series.

The seasonal adjustment procedure (X13-ARIMA-SEATS) is based on a model that estimates the monthly movements as percentages above or below the general level of series (unlike other methods that redistribute the actual series values over the calendar year). Because the data series for aircraft is highly variable, users studying data trends may wish to analyze aircraft separately from other trade.

ADJUSTMENTS FOR PRICE CHANGE

Data adjusted for seasonal variation on a real chained-dollar basis (2009 base year) are presented in Exhibits 10 and 11. This adjustment for price change is done using the Fisher chain-weighted methodology. The deflators are primarily based on the monthly price indexes published by the Bureau of Labor Statistics using techniques developed for the NIPAs by BEA.

PRINCIPAL COMMODITIES

Goods data appearing in Exhibit 15 are classified in terms of the SITC Revision 4, with the exception of agricultural and manufactured goods. Agricultural goods are defined by the U.S. Department of Agriculture (USDA); they consist of non-marine food products and other products of agriculture that have not passed through complex processes of manufacture. Manufactured goods conform to the NAICS; they consist of goods that have been mechanically, physically, or chemically transformed. USDA agricultural goods and NAICS manufactured goods are not mutually exclusive categories.

Re-exports are foreign merchandise entering the country as imports and then exported in substantially the same condition as when imported. Re-exports, included in overall export totals, appear as separate line items in Exhibit 15.

ADVANCED TECHNOLOGY PRODUCTS

About 500 of some 22,000 Schedule B and Harmonized Tariff Schedule classification codes used in reporting U.S. merchandise trade are identified as "advanced technology" codes, and they meet the following criteria:

1. The code contains products whose technology is from a recognized high technology field (e.g., biotechnology).

2. These products represent leading edge technology in that field.

3. Such products constitute a significant part of all items covered in the selected classification code.

The aggregation of the goods results in a measure of advanced technology trade that appears in Exhibits 16 and 16a. This product- and commodity-based measure of advanced technology differs from broader NAICS-based measures, which include all goods produced by a particular industry group, regardless of the level of technology embodied in the goods.

GOODS (BALANCE OF PAYMENTS BASIS) AND SERVICES

Quarterly and annual statistics for goods on a balance of payments (BOP) basis and for services are included in the U.S. International Transactions Accounts (ITAs), which are published by BEA in news releases in March, June, September, and December and in the *Survey of Current Business* in the January, April, July, and October issues. The next release of the ITAs is scheduled for June 18, 2015. The *Survey of Current Business* is available online at www.bea.gov/scb/index.htm.

GOODS (BALANCE OF PAYMENTS BASIS)

Goods on a Census basis are adjusted by BEA to a BOP basis to align the data with the concepts and definitions used to prepare the international and national economic accounts. These adjustments, which are applied separately to exports and imports, are necessary to supplement coverage of the Census data, to eliminate duplication of transactions recorded elsewhere in the international accounts, and to value transactions at market prices. They include both *additions* to and *deductions* from goods on a Census basis and are presented in this release as *net adjustments*. Adjustments that exhibit significant seasonal patterns are seasonally adjusted. BEA also publishes more detailed quarterly and annual statistics for *net adjustments* in ITA Table 2.4. U.S. International Trade in Goods, Balance of Payments Adjustments and in the January, April, July, and October issues of the *Survey of Current Business*.

The export adjustments include:

Exports under U.S. military sales contracts - This adjustment reflects the net amount of two separate adjustments. BEA first *deducts* goods identified in the Census data as exports under the U.S. Foreign Military Sales program. BEA then *adds* primary source data for these exports, which are reported to BEA by the U.S. Department of Defense.

Gold exports, nonmonetary - This *addition* is made for gold that is purchased by foreign official agencies from private dealers in the United States and held at the Federal Reserve Bank of New York. The Census data only include gold that leaves the U.S. customs territory.

Goods procured in U.S. ports by foreign carriers - This *addition* is made for foreign air and ocean carriers' fuel purchases in U.S. ports.

Net exports of goods under merchanting - This *addition* is made to include the net value of the purchase and subsequent resale of goods abroad without the goods entering the United States. Because these goods do not cross the U.S. customs frontier, their value is not recorded in the Census data.

Other adjustments to exports include:

Deductions for equipment repairs (parts and labor), developed motion picture film, and military grant-aid. *Additions* for sales of fish caught in U.S. territorial waters, exports of electricity to Mexico, private gift parcels, vessels and oil rigs for which ownership changes, valuation of software exports at market value, and low-value (below reporting threshold) transactions for 1999–2009 to phase in a revised Census Bureau low-value methodology that was implemented for goods on a Census basis beginning with statistics for 2010.

The import adjustments include:

Gold imports, nonmonetary - This *addition* is made for gold sold by foreign official agencies to private purchasers out of stock held at the Federal Reserve Bank of New York. The Census data only include gold that enters the U.S. customs territory.

Goods procured in foreign ports by U.S. carriers - This *addition* is made for U.S. air and ocean carriers' fuel purchases in foreign ports.

Imports by U.S. military agencies - This *addition* is made for purchases of goods abroad by U.S. military agencies, which are reported to BEA by the U.S. Department of Defense. The Census data only include imports of goods by U.S. military agencies that enter the U.S. customs territory.

Inland freight in Canada and Mexico - This *addition* is made for inland freight in Canada and Mexico. Imports of goods from all countries should be valued at the customs value—the value at the foreign port of export including inland freight charges. For imports from Canada and Mexico, this should be the cost of the goods at the U.S. border. However, the customs value for imports for certain Canadian and Mexican goods is the point of origin in Canada or Mexico. BEA makes an *addition* for the inland freight charges of transporting these goods to the U.S. border to make the value comparable to the customs value reported for imports from other countries.

Other adjustments to imports include:

Deductions for equipment repairs (parts and labor), repairs to U.S. vessels abroad, and developed motion picture film. *Additions* for non-reported imports of locomotives and railcars, imports of electricity from Mexico, conversion of vessels for commercial use, valuation of software imports at market value, and low-value (below reporting threshold) transactions for 1999–2009 to phase in a revised Census Bureau low-value methodology that was implemented for goods on a Census basis beginning with statistics for 2010.

SERVICES

The services statistics cover transactions between foreign countries and the 50 states, the District of Columbia, Puerto Rico, the U.S. Virgin Islands, and other U.S. territories and possessions. Transactions with U.S. military, diplomatic, and consular installations abroad are excluded because these installations are considered to be part of the U.S. economy.

Services statistics are based on quarterly, annual, and benchmark surveys and information obtained from monthly government and industry reports. For categories for which monthly data are not available, monthly statistics are derived from quarterly statistics through temporal distribution, or interpolation. The interpolation methodology used by BEA is the modified Denton proportional first difference method. This method preserves the pattern of the monthly indicator series, if available, while satisfying the annual aggregation constraints. See "An Empirical Review of Methods for Temporal Distribution and Interpolation in the National Accounts" for more information. Services are seasonally adjusted when statistically significant seasonal patterns are present.

Services are shown in nine broad categories. The following is a brief description of the types of services included in each category:

Maintenance and repair services n.i.e. (not included elsewhere) - Consists of maintenance and repair services performed by residents of one country on goods that are owned by residents of another country. The repairs may be performed at the site of the repair facility or elsewhere. Excludes such services in which the cost is included in the price of the goods and is not billed separately or is declared as a part of the price of the goods on the import or export declaration filed with the U.S. Customs and Border Protection. Maintenance and repair of ships, aircraft, and other transport equipment are included under transport services, and maintenance and repair of computers are included under computer services.

Transport - Consists of transactions associated with moving people and freight from one location to another and includes related supporting and auxiliary services. Transport covers all modes of transportation, including air, sea, rail, road, space, and pipeline. Postal and courier services and port services, which cover cargo handling, storage and warehousing, and other related transport services, are also included.

Travel (for all purposes including education) - Includes goods and services acquired by nonresidents while abroad. A traveler is defined as a person who stays, or intends to stay, for less than one year in a country of which he or she is not a resident or as a nonresident whose purpose is to obtain education or medical treatment, no matter how long the stay. Purchases can be either for own use or for gifts to others. Travel is a transactor-based component that covers a variety of goods and services, primarily lodging, meals, transportation in the country of travel, amusement, entertainment, and gifts. Excludes air passenger services for travel between countries, which are included in *transport*, and goods for resale, which are included in goods.

Travel includes business and personal travel. Business travel covers goods and services acquired for use by persons whose primary purpose for travel is for business (including goods and services for which business travelers are reimbursed by employers). Business travel also includes expenditures by border, seasonal, and other short-term workers in their economy of employment. Personal travel covers travel for all non-business purposes, including for medical or educational purposes.

Insurance services - Includes the direct insurance services of providing life insurance and annuities, non-life (property and casualty) insurance, reinsurance, freight insurance, and auxiliary insurance services. Insurance is measured as gross premiums earned plus premium supplements less claims payable, with an adjustment for claims volatility. Premium supplements represent investment income from insurance reserves, which are attributed to policyholders who are treated as paying the income back to the insurer. Auxiliary insurance services include agents' commissions, brokerage services, insurance consulting services, actuarial services, and other insurance services.

Financial services - Includes financial intermediary and auxiliary services, except insurance services. These services include those normally provided by banks and other financial institutions. Services primarily include those for which an explicit commission or a fee is charged; implicit fees for bond transactions, measured as the difference between bid and ask prices, are also included. Services include securities brokerage and underwriting, financial management, financial advisory, and custody services; credit and other credit-related services; and securities lending, electronic funds transfer, and other services.

Charges for the use of intellectual property n.i.e. - Includes charges for the use of proprietary rights, such as patents, trademarks, and copyrights, and charges for licenses to use, reproduce, distribute, and sell or purchase intellectual property.

Telecommunications, computer, and information services - Telecommunications services include the broadcast or transmission of sound, images, data, or other information by electronic means. These services do not include the value of the information transmitted. Computer services consist of hardware- and software-related services and data processing services. Sales of customized software and related use licenses, as well as licenses to use non-customized software with a periodic license fee, are also included, as is software downloaded or otherwise electronically delivered. Cross-border transactions in non-customized packaged software with a license for perpetual use are included in goods. Information services include news agency services, database services, and web search portals.

Other business services - Consists of research and development services, professional and management consulting services, and technical, trade-related, and other business services. Research and development services include services associated with basic and applied research and experimental development of new products and processes. Professional and management consulting services include legal services, accounting, management consulting, managerial services, public relations services, advertising, and market research. Amounts received by a parent company from its affiliates for general overhead expenses related to these services are included. Technical, trade-related, and other business services include architectural and engineering, construction, audio-visual, waste treatment, operational leasing, trade-related, and other business services.

Government goods and services n.i.e. - Includes goods and services supplied by and to enclaves, such as embassies, military bases, and international organizations; goods and services acquired from the host economy by diplomats, consular staff, and military personnel located abroad and their dependents; and services supplied by and to governments that are not included in other services categories. Services supplied by and to governments are classified to specific services categories when source data permit.

GOODS (BOP BASIS) AND SERVICES BY COUNTRY AND AREA

Monthly country and area detail is not available for goods on a BOP basis or for services. However, quarterly statistics on goods on a BOP basis and on services that are seasonally adjusted by geography are shown in Exhibit 20. Unlike the seasonal adjustments by commodity and by service type that are applied to the global totals, these adjustments are developed and applied directly at the country and world area levels. For total exports and imports, data users should refer to the by-commodity and by-service type totals shown in the other exhibits. The seasonally adjusted country and world area data will not sum to the seasonally adjusted by-commodity and by-service type totals because the two sets of statistics are derived from different aggregations of the export and import data and from different seasonal adjustment models. Data users should use caution drawing comparisons between the two sets of seasonally adjusted series.

The definitions of the world areas shown in Exhibit 20 are consistent with the definitions for goods on a Census basis (see *AREA GROUPINGS* above) with a few exceptions. For services, CAFTA-DR is not available because trade with this area's member countries cannot be separately identified. For goods on a BOP basis and for services, European Union and OPEC reflect the composition of the areas as they were at the time of reporting.

REVISION PROCEDURE (GOODS ON A BOP BASIS AND SERVICES)

Monthly Revisions: Each month, a preliminary estimate for the current month and a revised estimate for the immediately preceding month are released. After the initial revision, no further revisions are made to a month until more complete source data become available in March, June, September, and December.

Quarterly Revisions: The releases in March, June, September, and December contain revised estimates for the previous six months to incorporate more comprehensive and updated source data.

Annual Revisions: Each June, historical data are revised to incorporate newly available and revised source data, changes in definitions and classifications, and changes in estimation methods. Seasonally adjusted data are also revised to reflect recalculated seasonal and trading-day adjustments.

Other Revisions: The release in February contains revisions to goods for January through November of the most recent year and the release in March contains revisions to both goods and services for all months of the most recent year. These revisions result from forcing the seasonally adjusted months to equal the annual totals.

DATA AVAILABILITY

The U.S. International Trade in Goods and Services news release (FT-900) and the FT-900 Supplement are available at the following:

www.census.gov/ft900

www.bea.gov/newsreleases/international/trade/tradnewsrelease.htm

MONTHLY RELEASE SCHEDULE

Statistical Month	Date	Day
January	03-06-15	Friday
February	04-02-15	Thursday
March	05-05-15	Tuesday
April	06-03-15	Wednesday
May	07-07-15	Tuesday
June	08-05-15	Wednesday
July	09-03-15	Thursday
August	10-06-15	Tuesday
September	11-04-15	Wednesday
October	12-04-15	Friday

U.S. Census Bureau News

U.S. Department of Commerce • Washington, D.C. 20230

FOR IMMEDIATE RELEASE
8:30 A.M. EDT TUESDAY, MAY 5, 2015

For information contact:
Economic Indicators Division
Matthew Przybocki   (301) 763-3148
Maria Iseman   (301) 763-2311

FT-900 SUPPLEMENT
March 2015

Exhibit 1: Exports, Imports, and Balance of Goods by Selected NAICS-Based Product Code, Not Seasonally Adjusted: March 2015

In millions of dollars. Details may not equal total due to rounding. (X) Not Applicable. (-) Represents zero or less than one-half unit of measurement shown.

| NAICS-Based Product Code Description | Balance | | Exports | | Imports for Consumption (Customs Value) | | | |
| | | | | | Totals | | Calculated Duty | |
	March	Year-to-Date	March	Year-to-Date	March	Year-to-Date	March	Year-to-Date
GRAND TOTAL	**-61,969.4**	**-161,910.3**	**133,325.3**	**373,070.8**	**195,294.7**	**534,981.1**	**2,973.1**	**8,049.7**
Agricultural, Forestry & Fishery Products	990.8	4,376.2	6,374.0	19,708.2	5,383.1	15,332.0	6.0	18.5
(Domestic)								
Agricultural Products, Total	2,064.7	7,940.2	5,443.2	17,556.5	3,378.5	9,616.3	5.2	16.1
Livestock And Livestock Products	-449.7	-1,153.7	172.3	464.9	622.0	1,618.6	0.2	0.6
Forestry Products	23.4	52.3	246.4	625.5	223.0	573.1	0.2	0.6
Fish, Fresh Or Chilled; And Other Marine Products	-647.6	-2,462.7	512.0	1,061.3	1,159.6	3,524.0	0.3	1.2
Mining, Total	-6,725.0	-23,289.0	3,050.9	8,943.4	9,775.9	32,232.5	6.7	18.1
(Domestic)								
Oil And Gas	-7,553.9	-25,418.4	1,663.9	5,067.6	9,217.8	30,486.0	6.6	17.5
Minerals And Ores	828.9	2,129.4	1,387.0	3,875.8	558.1	1,746.4	0.1	0.6
Manufacturing, Total	-71,831.2	-189,087.9	99,219.5	273,956.7	171,050.7	462,846.3	2,948.1	7,991.2
(Domestic)								
Food And Kindred Products	525.5	1,786.0	5,790.9	16,031.7	5,265.5	14,245.8	81.5	205.2
Beverages And Tobacco	-1,188.3	-3,025.4	690.3	1,751.3	1,878.5	4,776.7	9.1	21.5
Textile And Fabrics	45.5	212.9	818.7	2,260.4	773.1	2,047.5	36.7	98.7
Textile Mill Products	-1,603.2	-4,170.1	243.8	679.8	1,847.0	4,850.0	117.3	308.1
Apparel And Accessories	-7,044.3	-19,992.1	273.0	754.6	7,317.3	20,746.7	958.7	2,760.4
Leather And Allied Products	-3,233.2	-9,089.1	289.1	752.8	3,522.3	9,841.9	362.9	1,006.7
Wood Products	-948.6	-2,433.8	593.7	1,652.0	1,542.2	4,085.8	15.3	40.5
Paper Products	216.0	894.4	2,034.4	5,805.7	1,818.4	4,911.3	4.2	11.1
Printing, Publishing & Similar Products	-15.0	50.6	417.0	1,205.0	431.9	1,154.4	0.1	0.5
Petroleum And Coal Products	414.7	1,290.6	6,231.9	19,530.5	5,817.2	18,239.9	10.1	30.2
Chemicals	-3,240.5	-6,460.8	16,120.1	46,261.3	19,360.6	52,722.0	162.5	432.9
Plastic And Rubber Products (1)	-1,765.3	-4,346.3	2,681.7	7,375.8	4,446.9	11,722.0	110.8	287.8
Nonmetallic Mineral Products (1)	-878.8	-2,327.3	980.7	2,662.4	1,859.5	4,989.7	60.2	158.3
Primary Metal Products	-3,263.6	-10,716.3	4,949.0	14,009.2	8,212.5	24,725.5	30.1	80.3
Fabricated Metal Products	-2,567.4	-5,883.7	3,707.5	10,453.7	6,274.9	16,337.4	141.5	358.0
Machinery, Except Electrical	-3,593.6	-7,607.7	11,636.0	31,604.8	15,229.6	39,212.5	120.7	300.7
Computers and Electronic Products (1)	-19,896.0	-53,412.7	10,852.7	29,553.2	30,748.7	82,965.9	86.5	217.9
Electrical Equipment, Appliances and Components (1)	-4,628.7	-11,781.5	4,218.8	11,625.8	8,847.5	23,407.3	158.2	414.8
Transportation Equipment (1)	-10,909.1	-29,643.3	22,103.8	57,589.1	33,012.8	87,232.4	368.8	959.0
Furniture and Fixtures	-2,904.0	-7,566.4	449.3	1,211.6	3,353.3	8,778.0	6.0	15.8
Miscellaneous Manufactured Commodities	-5,353.6	-14,667.7	4,137.3	11,186.0	9,490.9	25,853.7	106.8	282.7
Special Classification Provisions	-2,970.5	-6,976.0	6,114.5	17,594.4	9,085.0	24,570.3	12.3	21.9
(Domestic)								
Scrap & Waste	1,068.4	2,889.2	1,504.5	4,276.7	436.1	1,387.6	0.1	0.2
Used Or Second-Hand Merchandise (1)	(-)	(-)	(-)	(-)	(-)	(-)	(-)	(-)
Goods Returned Or Reimported	-6,484.5	-16,861.6	1.4	8.4	6,486.0	16,870.0	0.2	0.7
Special Classification Provision, Nspf	2,369.4	6,899.8	3,597.3	10,313.0	1,227.9	3,413.1	10.7	17.2
Re-exports	18,566.5	53,023.7	18,566.5	53,023.7	(X)	(X)	(X)	(X)
Timing Adjustments	(X)	42.7	(X)	42.7	(X)	(X)	(X)	(X)

(1) Due to non-disclosure requirements, certain 10-digit Schedule B commodity classifications are subject to suppression and require a change in aggregation. For additional information see www.census.gov/ft900.

Exhibit 2. Origin of Movement of U. S. Exports of Goods by State by NAICS-Based Product Code Groupings, Not Seasonally Adjusted: 2015

In millions of dollars. Foreign Trade Zone (FTZ) shipments are included in the U. S. total and distributed among individual states and territories. Separate FTZ total line is for reference only. Details may not equal totals due to rounding. (X) Not applicable. (-) Represents zero or less than one-half unit of measurement shown.

Item	NAICS-Based Product Code Groupings						Re-exports		Total	
	Manufactured Commodities			Non-Manufactured Commodities (1)						
	March	Year-to-Date		March	Year-to-Date		March	Year-to-Date	March	Year-to-Date
		Total	Percent		Total	Percent				
U.S. Total	99,219.5	273,956.7	100.0	13,220.8	39,719.5	100.0	18,566.5	53,023.7	133,325.3	373,070.8
Foreign Trade Zone	2,978.8	7,900.6	2.9	0.0	0.2	(-)	211.5	647.9	3,190.3	8,548.7
Alabama	1,611.1	4,096.6	1.5	135.8	448.1	1.1	79.0	166.1	1,825.9	4,710.8
Alaska	28.1	108.7	(-)	411.0	693.8	1.7	5.2	12.0	444.3	814.4
Arizona	1,210.6	3,307.5	1.2	422.9	1,169.6	2.9	412.0	1,318.3	2,045.5	5,795.3
Arkansas	390.1	1,150.3	0.4	40.9	121.1	0.3	20.2	91.5	451.3	1,363.0
California	9,701.6	25,790.3	9.4	2,014.7	4,973.6	12.5	3,262.5	9,434.2	14,978.9	40,198.1
Colorado	640.0	1,681.2	0.6	35.6	105.9	0.3	91.7	242.0	767.4	2,029.2
Connecticut	1,241.2	3,550.3	1.3	49.6	139.0	0.3	85.6	245.5	1,376.5	3,934.8
Delaware	292.1	829.2	0.3	11.1	25.0	0.1	117.6	303.7	420.8	1,157.9
Florida	3,644.9	9,956.4	3.6	408.0	1,053.4	2.7	904.4	2,601.2	4,957.3	13,611.0
Georgia	2,914.7	7,796.8	2.8	275.9	794.6	2.0	276.8	749.2	3,467.3	9,340.6
Hawaii	61.7	387.5	0.1	17.0	42.6	0.1	2.6	10.9	81.4	440.9
Idaho	234.0	656.5	0.2	51.7	141.9	0.4	112.4	338.4	398.1	1,136.8
Illinois	4,330.5	11,914.4	4.3	378.3	1,453.0	3.7	931.1	2,416.5	5,639.9	15,784.0
Indiana	2,791.0	7,762.3	2.8	40.0	129.6	0.3	212.4	603.0	3,043.4	8,494.9
Iowa	1,026.1	2,728.8	1.0	103.9	445.8	1.1	49.3	140.0	1,179.2	3,314.6
Kansas	791.6	2,027.2	0.7	153.4	486.7	1.2	64.0	186.4	1,009.0	2,700.3
Kentucky	2,123.5	5,680.1	2.1	17.2	72.8	0.2	423.7	1,292.9	2,564.4	7,045.8
Louisiana	2,660.8	8,051.9	2.9	950.0	4,669.3	11.8	34.1	94.8	3,644.9	12,816.0
Maine	137.1	400.8	0.1	60.1	175.3	0.4	12.1	28.3	209.2	604.4
Maryland	634.2	1,708.4	0.6	79.5	198.8	0.5	178.0	487.2	891.8	2,394.4
Massachusetts	1,819.4	4,862.1	1.8	90.8	280.1	0.7	315.4	912.2	2,225.6	6,054.3
Michigan	3,901.9	10,569.7	3.9	354.8	992.6	2.5	451.6	1,319.9	4,708.3	12,882.1
Minnesota	1,555.6	4,215.5	1.5	81.8	248.2	0.6	158.7	398.6	1,796.1	4,862.3
Mississippi	763.0	2,203.5	0.8	66.3	200.2	0.5	114.0	324.6	943.3	2,728.3
Missouri	1,005.9	2,822.0	1.0	89.2	274.9	0.7	83.7	227.2	1,178.8	3,324.0
Montana	82.1	227.1	0.1	29.2	88.9	0.2	4.3	12.2	115.6	328.3
Nebraska	524.7	1,427.1	0.5	79.5	218.8	0.6	47.7	92.0	651.8	1,737.9
Nevada	474.9	1,485.9	0.5	53.9	101.1	0.3	106.6	331.9	635.3	1,918.8
New Hampshire	297.3	741.0	0.3	15.3	35.9	0.1	51.9	190.0	364.5	966.9
New Jersey	2,089.1	5,526.4	2.0	249.9	721.0	1.8	506.4	1,591.9	2,845.5	7,839.3
New Mexico	199.4	535.6	0.2	14.4	30.1	0.1	113.9	312.8	327.7	878.5
New York	4,185.8	10,818.5	3.9	922.3	2,979.6	7.5	2,537.2	7,499.9	7,645.3	21,298.1
North Carolina	2,257.9	6,286.5	2.3	296.6	681.1	1.7	229.1	641.0	2,783.6	7,608.5
North Dakota	169.3	436.8	0.2	234.8	636.4	1.6	10.2	24.2	414.3	1,097.4
Ohio	3,925.5	10,432.1	3.8	211.7	705.6	1.8	377.7	1,071.7	4,515.0	12,209.4
Oklahoma	410.3	1,159.8	0.4	30.9	79.4	0.2	110.4	184.4	551.7	1,423.6
Oregon	1,422.6	3,915.8	1.4	209.8	687.7	1.7	231.8	606.4	1,864.2	5,209.9
Pennsylvania	2,807.4	7,667.0	2.8	286.2	759.7	1.9	589.3	1,488.0	3,682.8	9,914.6
Rhode Island	124.6	330.7	0.1	47.1	153.8	0.4	12.9	42.3	184.6	526.8
South Carolina	2,171.5	6,215.5	2.3	54.2	186.6	0.5	114.2	437.3	2,339.9	6,839.3
South Dakota	106.5	334.8	0.1	4.7	18.0	(-)	1.9	4.4	113.1	357.3
Tennessee	2,064.3	5,784.7	2.1	137.9	365.3	0.9	608.7	1,630.4	2,810.9	7,780.4
Texas	15,784.9	45,946.2	16.8	1,369.9	5,292.0	13.3	3,716.8	10,584.6	21,371.6	61,822.9
Utah	946.6	2,886.6	1.1	69.1	183.2	0.5	48.5	165.5	1,064.2	3,235.3
Vermont	219.5	597.8	0.2	7.5	19.7	(-)	80.5	224.2	307.6	841.8
Virginia	1,280.6	3,530.2	1.3	220.2	769.3	1.9	168.0	449.2	1,668.9	4,748.7
Washington	6,698.6	17,010.0	6.2	1,204.1	3,611.0	9.1	244.7	715.7	8,147.4	21,336.8
West Virginia	332.9	969.3	0.4	198.2	540.0	1.4	15.3	62.2	546.4	1,571.5
Wisconsin	1,864.3	4,837.0	1.8	99.3	317.5	0.8	159.1	436.3	2,122.6	5,590.8
Wyoming	95.1	297.4	0.1	4.7	12.5	(-)	2.3	7.1	102.1	316.9
Dist of Columbia	32.6	118.2	(-)	9.2	17.5	(-)	1.1	4.5	42.9	140.2
Puerto Rico	1,522.1	5,619.3	2.1	10.8	40.1	0.1	66.7	229.1	1,599.5	5,888.5
US Virgin Islands	2.5	69.8	(-)	0.1	0.6	(-)	10.1	37.1	12.6	107.5
Other	1,615.5	4,491.6	1.6	309.9	1,131.4	2.8	1.2	3.0	4,245.1	11,954.0
Estimated Shipments	(X)	(X)	(X)	(X)	(X)	(X)	(X)	(X)	2,318.6	6,526.4
Unreported (2)	1,615.5	4,491.6	1.6	309.9	1,131.4	2.8	1.2	3.0	1,926.5	5,427.6
Timing Adjustment	(X)	(X)	(X)	(X)	(X)	(X)	(X)	(X)	(X)	42.7

(1) Includes agricultural, forestry, fishery products, mineral commodities, scrap, waste and used or second-hand merchandise. The state of origin of movement value totals for non-manufactured commodities usually reflect the state where the U.S. port of export is located.

(2) Includes prior month's revision to exports to Canada.

Exhibit 2a. U. S. General Imports of Goods by State, State of Destination, by NAICS-Based Product Code Groupings, Not Seasonally Adjusted: 2015

In millions of dollars. Foreign Trade Zone (FTZ) shipments are included in the U. S. total and distributed among individual states and territories. Separate FTZ total line is for reference only. Details may not equal totals due to rounding. (X) Not applicable. (-) Represents zero or less than one-half unit of measurement shown.

Item	NAICS-Based Product Code Groupings						Total		
	Manufactured Commodities			Non-Manufactured Commodities (1)					
	March	Year-to-Date		March	Year-to-Date		March	Year-to-Date	
		Total	Percent		Total	Percent		Total	Percent
U.S. Total	171,178.5	461,033.3	100.0	25,454.5	75,342.3	100.0	197,500.4	539,860.2	100.0
Foreign Trade Zone	13,853.6	35,485.2	7.7	6,401.0	19,499.8	25.9	20,254.6	54,985.0	10.2
Alabama	1,691.5	4,755.5	1.0	248.9	736.6	1.0	1,940.4	5,492.1	1.0
Alaska	116.2	368.1	0.1	40.2	87.1	0.1	156.4	455.2	0.1
Arizona	1,275.7	3,559.4	0.8	419.1	1,314.1	1.7	1,694.8	4,873.4	0.9
Arkansas	660.5	1,665.1	0.4	13.7	44.5	0.1	674.2	1,709.7	0.3
California	31,892.0	82,804.7	18.0	3,300.0	9,916.1	13.2	35,192.1	92,720.8	17.2
Colorado	922.8	2,534.6	0.5	227.1	717.9	1.0	1,149.8	3,252.5	0.6
Connecticut	1,571.7	4,821.4	1.0	226.1	730.6	1.0	1,797.8	5,552.0	1.0
Delaware	496.7	1,756.8	0.4	278.7	686.0	0.9	775.4	2,442.8	0.5
Florida	5,310.8	14,886.9	3.2	994.6	3,096.6	4.1	6,305.3	17,983.6	3.3
Georgia	7,755.9	21,025.6	4.6	230.3	607.3	0.8	7,986.2	21,632.9	4.0
Hawaii	117.1	427.3	0.1	169.5	528.8	0.7	286.6	956.1	0.2
Idaho	450.8	1,241.5	0.3	28.1	70.9	0.1	478.9	1,312.4	0.2
Illinois	8,863.2	23,066.4	5.0	1,978.4	6,972.9	9.3	10,841.6	30,039.3	5.6
Indiana	4,520.2	11,841.4	2.6	220.1	594.4	0.8	4,740.3	12,435.8	2.3
Iowa	816.7	2,152.5	0.5	109.3	359.8	0.5	926.1	2,512.3	0.5
Kansas	960.2	2,376.6	0.5	146.2	333.9	0.4	1,106.4	2,710.5	0.5
Kentucky	3,234.2	8,512.7	1.8	173.3	587.2	0.8	3,407.5	9,099.9	1.7
Louisiana	1,199.8	3,839.9	0.8	1,612.5	4,674.6	6.2	2,812.3	8,514.5	1.6
Maine	265.9	728.0	0.2	82.0	238.1	0.3	347.9	966.1	0.2
Maryland	2,824.0	7,226.6	1.6	146.6	410.4	0.5	2,970.6	7,637.1	1.4
Massachusetts	2,360.1	6,616.2	1.4	508.0	1,345.4	1.8	2,868.1	7,961.6	1.5
Michigan	10,391.1	26,888.7	5.8	645.0	1,936.1	2.6	11,036.0	28,824.8	5.3
Minnesota	2,045.3	5,347.5	1.2	551.0	1,688.1	2.2	2,596.2	7,035.6	1.3
Mississippi	931.8	2,438.3	0.5	259.4	791.3	1.1	1,191.2	3,229.5	0.6
Missouri	1,525.0	3,994.1	0.9	125.8	297.0	0.4	1,650.8	4,291.0	0.8
Montana	92.4	237.8	0.1	225.9	819.2	1.1	318.3	1,056.9	0.2
Nebraska	334.6	946.2	0.2	54.3	115.1	0.2	388.9	1,061.3	0.2
Nevada	706.3	1,657.6	0.4	21.0	59.9	0.1	727.3	1,717.5	0.3
New Hampshire	920.8	2,416.9	0.5	36.1	110.6	0.1	957.0	2,527.5	0.5
New Jersey	9,234.2	24,756.7	5.4	1,371.7	3,319.2	4.4	10,605.9	28,076.0	5.2
New Mexico	168.4	481.7	0.1	19.4	58.7	0.1	187.8	540.3	0.1
New York	9,611.7	26,454.8	5.7	2,596.9	6,259.5	8.3	12,208.6	32,714.3	6.1
North Carolina	4,276.9	11,680.5	2.5	179.7	794.4	1.1	4,456.6	12,474.9	2.3
North Dakota	222.9	587.3	0.1	117.6	299.2	0.4	340.5	886.5	0.2
Ohio	5,710.0	15,184.9	3.3	428.5	1,507.5	2.0	6,138.5	16,692.4	3.1
Oklahoma	646.1	1,776.4	0.4	367.3	1,014.2	1.3	1,013.5	2,790.5	0.5
Oregon	1,211.1	3,499.8	0.8	134.6	384.5	0.5	1,345.8	3,884.3	0.7
Pennsylvania	6,838.7	17,964.6	3.9	764.8	1,800.6	2.4	7,603.5	19,765.3	3.7
Rhode Island	647.2	1,773.9	0.4	24.1	69.0	0.1	671.3	1,842.8	0.3
South Carolina	3,307.4	9,468.4	2.1	107.3	319.0	0.4	3,414.7	9,787.4	1.8
South Dakota	120.6	309.8	0.1	12.5	35.9	(-)	133.1	345.7	0.1
Tennessee	6,376.3	17,146.7	3.7	351.0	992.0	1.3	6,727.3	18,138.7	3.4
Texas	17,918.9	50,683.8	11.0	4,160.0	13,293.0	17.6	22,078.9	63,976.9	11.9
Utah	998.5	2,667.5	0.6	67.8	226.3	0.3	1,066.3	2,893.7	0.5
Vermont	257.3	747.0	0.2	115.1	350.2	0.5	372.4	1,097.2	0.2
Virginia	2,069.6	5,551.6	1.2	196.0	548.4	0.7	2,265.6	6,100.0	1.1
Washington	3,497.7	9,534.4	2.1	983.9	3,032.4	4.0	4,481.5	12,566.8	2.3
West Virginia	366.5	923.5	0.2	9.4	31.4	(-)	375.9	954.9	0.2
Wisconsin	1,968.2	5,221.1	1.1	104.6	333.6	0.4	2,072.8	5,554.7	1.0
Wyoming	54.1	151.4	(-)	51.1	137.5	0.2	105.2	288.8	0.1
Dist of Columbia	39.3	130.8	(-)	64.7	257.1	0.3	104.1	387.9	0.1
Puerto Rico	1,337.1	4,068.9	0.9	130.9	366.3	0.5	1,468.0	4,435.2	0.8
US Virgin Islands	7.0	44.6	(-)	3.0	7.3	(-)	10.0	51.9	(-)
Other	39.4	89.2	(-)	21.5	34.7	(-)	928.3	2,510.0	0.5
Estimated Shipments	(X)	(X)	(X)	(X)	(X)	(X)	867.4	2,386.2	0.4
Unreported	39.4	89.2	(-)	21.5	34.7	(-)	60.9	123.9	(-)
Timing Adjustment	(X)	(X)	(X)	(X)	(X)	(X)	(X)	1,098.3	(X)

(1) Includes agricultural, forestry, fishery products, mineral commodities, scrap, waste and used or second-hand merchandise.

Exhibit 3. Exports, Imports, and Trade Balance of Goods

In millions of dollars. Details may not equal totals due to seasonal adjustment and rounding.(R) - Revised.

Period	Balance		Exports F.A.S. Value	Imports	
	Customs	C.I.F.		Customs value	C.I.F. Value
Seasonally Adjusted					
2014					
Jan.- Dec.	-721,577.1	-786,187.8	1,623,196.8	2,344,773.9	2,409,384.6
Jan.- Mar.	-177,092.4	-192,988.4	397,480.1	574,572.5	590,468.5
January	-58,442.3	-63,728.8	132,268.7	190,711.0	195,997.5
February	-57,749.7	-62,941.7	130,479.9	188,229.6	193,421.6
March	-60,900.4	-66,317.9	134,731.5	195,631.9	201,049.4
April	-64,318.2	-69,691.8	134,192.6	198,510.9	203,884.4
May	-61,882.4	-67,231.7	135,968.0	197,850.4	203,199.7
June	-59,278.5	-64,584.0	135,831.8	195,110.3	200,415.7
July	-58,377.6	-63,681.5	138,069.5	196,447.1	201,751.0
August	-58,231.2	-63,594.6	138,508.9	196,740.1	202,103.5
September	-60,951.0	-66,344.6	135,594.5	196,545.5	201,939.1
October	-60,045.8	-65,558.9	138,004.4	198,050.2	203,563.3
November	-57,927.3	-63,403.4	135,859.5	193,786.8	199,262.9
December	-63,472.7	-69,109.0	133,687.4	197,160.1	202,796.3
2015					
Jan.- Mar.	-185,849.9	-203,317.2	378,440.5	564,290.4	581,757.7
January	-61,518.2	-67,117.4	127,629.7	189,147.9	194,747.1
February (R)	-54,569.5	-60,118.1	124,780.3	179,349.8	184,898.4
March	-69,762.2	-76,081.7	126,030.4	195,792.6	202,112.2
April					
May					
June					
July					
August					
September					
October					
November					
December					
Not Seasonally Adjusted					
2014					
Jan.- Dec.	-721,577.1	-786,187.8	1,623,196.8	2,344,773.9	2,409,384.6
Jan.- Mar.	-154,571.6	-169,874.5	393,141.3	547,712.9	563,015.8
January	-57,193.1	-62,436.1	127,508.3	184,701.4	189,944.4
February	-45,937.2	-50,670.8	123,727.8	169,665.1	174,398.6
March	-51,441.3	-56,767.7	141,905.2	193,346.4	198,672.8
April	-66,700.0	-72,170.7	133,817.2	200,517.1	205,987.9
May	-61,852.2	-67,314.7	138,224.9	200,077.1	205,539.6
June	-59,046.4	-64,415.8	138,399.8	197,446.2	202,815.6
July	-70,762.2	-76,335.9	133,490.7	204,252.9	209,826.6
August	-58,657.2	-64,057.1	137,878.4	196,535.6	201,935.6
September	-69,389.5	-74,885.6	133,424.8	202,814.3	208,310.4
October	-64,907.1	-70,699.1	145,828.8	210,735.9	216,527.9
November	-54,603.2	-59,856.2	135,190.8	189,794.0	195,047.0
December	-61,087.8	-66,578.2	133,800.2	194,887.9	200,378.3
2015					
Jan.- Mar.	-166,789.4	-183,621.0	373,070.8	539,860.2	556,691.7
January	-58,715.5	-64,173.4	121,397.9	180,113.5	185,571.3
February (R)	-43,898.8	-48,968.5	118,347.5	162,246.3	167,316.0
March	-64,175.1	-70,479.1	133,325.3	197,500.4	203,804.5
April					
May					
June					
July					
August					
September					
October					
November					
December					

Exhibit 4. Exports, Imports, and Trade Balance by Country and Area, Not Seasonally Adjusted: 2015

In millions of dollars. Details may not equal totals due to rounding. (X) Not applicable. (-) Represents zero or less than one-half unit of measurement shown.

Country	Balance (Customs imports)			Exports Domestic & Foreign, F.A.S. basis			Imports Customs basis			Imports C.I.F. basis		
	March	Year-to-Date	Rank	March	Year-to-Date	Rank	March	Year-to-Date	Rank	March	Year-to-Date	Rank
TOTAL	-64,175.1	-166,789.4	(X)	133,325.3	373,070.8	(X)	197,500.4	539,860.2	(X)	203,804.5	556,691.7	(X)
Afghanistan	88.4	160.2	198	89.7	168.7	88	1.3	8.4	151	1.3	9.0	151
Albania	1.3	-21.8	69	3.8	8.2	169	2.5	29.9	118	3.2	31.5	118
Algeria	-1.9	-278.3	44	151.5	403.2	66	153.4	681.4	59	161.7	717.8	59
Andorra	0.1	0.5	113	0.2	0.6	209	0.1	0.2	206	0.1	0.2	207
Angola	-119.3	-311.2	43	101.1	296.3	73	220.4	607.5	61	228.3	633.7	61
Anguilla	3.2	8.2	145	3.4	9.4	166	0.3	1.3	175	0.3	1.3	175
Antigua and Barbuda	122.8	290.4	209	122.9	290.9	76	0.1	0.6	187	0.1	0.6	188
Argentina	506.2	1,253.0	225	842.0	2,205.1	30	335.8	952.1	53	356.4	1,003.3	53
Armenia	-3.5	-8.1	76	3.5	10.0	162	7.0	18.2	127	7.4	19.1	128
Aruba	60.5	291.4	210	63.2	296.5	72	2.7	5.2	158	2.7	5.2	158
Australia	1,246.5	3,309.5	230	2,161.5	5,926.1	15	915.1	2,616.6	30	941.5	2,692.8	30
Austria	-818.1	-688.2	30	215.4	2,042.8	32	1,033.4	2,731.1	29	1,058.0	2,793.7	29
Azerbaijan	-16.4	-97.5	50	21.8	70.0	114	38.2	167.5	80	40.6	170.3	80
Bahamas	280.1	540.4	218	318.8	647.8	53	38.7	107.4	91	40.8	113.4	91
Bahrain	11.1	55.9	184	98.7	328.5	70	87.7	272.6	74	91.8	286.1	75
Bangladesh	-460.6	-1,329.7	20	88.0	204.6	84	548.6	1,534.3	38	570.2	1,593.6	37
Barbados	28.7	116.1	193	32.7	131.8	94	4.0	15.7	136	4.1	16.1	135
Belarus	-17.7	-62.4	58	5.0	12.1	160	22.7	74.5	100	23.0	77.4	99
Belgium	1,281.3	3,918.2	231	2,917.1	8,446.6	11	1,635.8	4,528.4	21	1,677.5	4,649.3	23
Belize	21.4	52.0	183	28.5	68.1	117	7.1	16.2	134	7.6	17.4	132
Benin	56.1	177.3	200	56.8	179.2	87	0.6	1.9	167	0.6	2.0	168
Bermuda	162.2	188.1	202	163.2	263.7	77	1.0	75.7	99	1.1	75.8	101
Bhutan	0.1	0.4	110	0.1	0.4	215	0.0	0.0	222	0.0	0.0	222
Bolivia	-0.9	-69.2	55	86.3	216.1	82	87.2	285.3	72	88.0	287.2	74
Bosnia and Herzegovina	-4.3	-11.7	73	0.6	3.7	185	5.0	15.5	137	5.2	16.0	136
Botswana	-14.6	-34.8	66	3.9	9.8	164	18.4	44.6	112	18.8	46.1	113
Brazil	600.1	1,764.2	227	2,804.6	8,475.4	10	2,204.5	6,711.3	17	2,282.8	6,942.5	17
British Indian Ocean Territories	-1.2	-2.6	85	0.0	0.3	218	1.2	2.9	162	1.3	3.0	162
British Virgin Islands	15.0	41.8	176	15.8	43.7	133	0.8	2.0	166	0.8	2.0	166
Brunei	11.4	42.0	177	12.7	51.2	124	1.2	9.3	150	1.3	9.8	150
Bulgaria	-32.1	-72.6	54	24.5	69.9	115	56.6	142.5	86	59.8	149.1	84
Burkina Faso	4.2	8.8	147	4.4	9.7	165	0.2	0.9	183	0.2	0.9	183
Burma	1.6	19.0	158	11.6	45.2	128	9.9	26.2	122	10.3	27.3	121
Burundi	0.4	0.1	102	1.0	1.9	196	0.6	1.8	169	0.6	1.8	169
Cabo Verde	0.6	1.1	120	0.6	1.5	198	0.0	0.4	196	0.0	0.4	196
Cambodia	-256.2	-639.3	32	35.2	86.0	109	291.4	725.2	58	303.8	754.9	58
Cameroon	-2.1	8.2	146	11.6	55.3	123	13.7	47.1	109	14.5	50.7	109
Canada	-762.4	-5,112.3	10	25,034.5	69,347.0	1	25,796.9	74,459.4	2	26,420.0	76,330.7	2
Cayman Islands	46.0	137.7	195	52.4	147.4	91	6.4	9.7	149	6.4	9.8	149
Central African Republic	0.4	0.6	114	0.5	0.8	206	0.1	0.2	208	0.1	0.2	208
Chad	-101.1	-348.0	42	5.1	18.2	153	106.2	366.3	66	109.7	373.4	68
Chile	423.4	1,258.7	226	1,439.5	4,092.1	21	1,016.1	2,833.5	28	1,130.3	3,119.4	28
China	-31,234.7	-82,381.3	1	9,887.2	28,139.1	3	41,121.9	110,520.4	1	43,006.2	115,490.7	1
Christmas Island	-0.1	-0.1	93	(-)	0.3	217	0.1	0.5	192	0.1	0.5	192
Cocos (Keeling) Islands	-0.1	-0.4	90	0.0	0.0	229	0.1	0.4	195	0.1	0.4	194
Colombia	24.1	483.8	216	1,523.2	4,137.3	20	1,499.0	3,653.5	26	1,564.1	3,822.4	26
Comoros	0.1	0.0	99	0.1	0.2	220	0.0	0.2	205	0.0	0.2	205
Congo (Brazzaville)	-17.9	-50.6	64	64.1	100.3	101	81.9	150.9	83	83.6	156.2	82
Congo (Kinshasa)	8.0	18.0	156	16.5	50.6	125	8.5	32.6	117	8.6	33.2	117
Cook Islands	0.1	0.8	116	0.3	1.1	202	0.1	0.4	198	0.2	0.4	198
Costa Rica	151.0	320.1	211	556.5	1,494.4	39	405.4	1,174.3	44	426.0	1,231.9	44
Cote d'Ivoire	-103.9	-271.1	45	24.6	89.1	108	128.5	360.2	68	133.8	373.9	67
Croatia	-9.3	-53.9	62	44.9	98.5	103	54.2	152.4	82	55.8	156.0	83
Cuba	33.8	73.8	189	33.8	73.8	111	(-)	(-)	(X)	(-)	(-)	(X)
Curacao	14.2	48.0	182	60.1	129.2	96	45.9	81.2	97	46.4	82.2	97
Cyprus	29.8	37.8	175	32.2	45.1	129	2.5	7.4	153	2.6	7.8	154
Czech Republic	-210.2	-601.6	33	174.5	497.8	59	384.7	1,099.3	49	397.7	1,135.6	50
Denmark	-658.8	-1,466.6	19	183.1	552.8	56	841.9	2,019.4	34	853.2	2,047.1	35
Djibouti	12.4	23.4	166	14.8	39.7	137	2.4	16.3	133	2.4	16.4	134
Dominica	5.4	16.3	153	5.6	16.7	155	0.2	0.4	194	0.2	0.4	195
Dominican Republic	207.6	699.8	220	624.5	1,744.1	37	416.8	1,044.2	51	427.9	1,071.9	52
Ecuador	-139.0	-794.6	25	514.6	1,453.8	40	653.5	2,248.4	33	691.1	2,384.4	32
Egypt	241.3	727.4	221	363.3	1,093.4	45	122.0	366.0	67	128.8	386.5	66
El Salvador	38.6	154.6	197	266.5	756.6	51	227.9	602.0	62	234.8	620.3	62
Equatorial Guinea	10.8	31.0	172	10.9	44.0	132	0.2	13.1	139	0.2	13.8	139
Eritrea	0.1	0.4	112	0.1	0.5	212	0.0	0.0	220	0.0	0.0	221

Exhibit 4. Exports, Imports, and Trade Balance by Country and Area, Not Seasonally Adjusted: 2015

In millions of dollars. Details may not equal totals due to rounding. (✗) Not applicable. (-) Represents zero or less than one-half unit of measurement shown.

Country	Balance (Customs imports)			Exports Domestic & Foreign, F.A.S. basis			Imports Customs basis			Imports C.I.F. basis		
	March	Year-to-Date	Rank	March	Year-to-Date	Rank	March	Year-to-Date	Rank	March	Year-to-Date	Rank
Estonia	-24.9	-56.5	61	24.0	65.5	120	48.9	122.0	89	50.5	125.5	89
Ethiopia	30.4	178.3	201	40.3	207.7	83	9.8	29.4	119	10.3	30.7	119
Falkland Islands (Islas Malvinas)	-3.5	-4.4	82	0.4	0.6	210	3.9	5.0	159	3.9	5.1	159
Faroe Islands	-7.2	-16.7	71	0.7	1.0	204	7.9	17.7	131	10.9	24.6	123
Fiji	-12.4	-27.2	68	5.4	14.0	158	17.8	41.1	113	20.1	49.1	110
Finland	-277.8	-765.6	27	125.2	380.3	68	403.0	1,145.9	47	416.7	1,187.2	46
France	-1,568.1	-3,593.6	14	2,593.8	7,556.0	12	4,161.9	11,149.6	8	4,230.9	11,330.6	9
French Guiana	1.7	131.3	194	1.7	131.3	95	0.0	0.0	223	0.0	0.0	223
French Polynesia	11.6	26.1	168	14.4	34.3	140	2.8	8.3	152	3.1	8.9	152
French Southern and Antarctic Lands	0.5	2.4	128	0.5	2.4	192	(-)	0.0	224	(-)	0.0	224
Gabon	-49.0	-40.9	65	15.5	48.6	126	64.5	89.5	93	67.5	94.3	93
Gambia	4.2	8.9	148	4.2	8.9	167	0.0	0.1	213	0.0	0.1	212
Gaza Strip Administered by Israel	0.0	0.1	101	0.0	0.1	227	(-)	(-)	(X)	(-)	(-)	(X)
Georgia	11.4	45.0	179	27.6	95.2	105	16.2	50.2	108	16.5	52.1	108
Germany	-6,095.1	-16,698.8	3	4,667.3	12,482.5	6	10,762.4	29,181.3	5	10,979.0	29,748.7	5
Ghana	56.9	139.4	196	78.4	195.6	86	21.5	56.2	106	23.0	60.4	106
Gibraltar	187.1	491.7	217	187.1	491.8	60	0.0	0.0	216	0.0	0.0	216
Greece	-51.7	-78.2	53	54.5	200.7	85	106.2	278.8	73	112.6	295.5	72
Greenland	2.6	2.7	129	2.9	3.2	187	0.3	0.5	190	0.3	0.5	190
Grenada	5.3	21.5	160	6.3	23.4	145	0.9	1.9	168	1.0	2.0	167
Guadeloupe	3.9	32.7	173	4.0	33.4	141	0.1	0.7	184	0.1	0.7	185
Guatemala	117.0	359.0	214	496.0	1,407.4	41	379.1	1,048.3	50	416.1	1,138.0	49
Guinea	29.5	26.2	169	38.8	44.1	131	9.3	17.9	129	12.2	24.5	124
Guinea-Bissau	0.1	0.4	111	0.2	0.4	214	0.0	0.0	219	0.0	0.0	219
Guyana	-8.8	0.3	106	38.2	116.9	98	47.0	116.6	90	47.5	118.2	90
Haiti	27.5	56.6	185	107.9	256.0	79	80.4	199.4	78	81.9	203.3	78
Heard and McDonald Islands	0.1	0.7	115	0.1	0.7	208	(-)	0.0	227	(-)	0.0	227
Honduras	-22.9	166.2	199	432.0	1,321.6	43	454.8	1,155.4	45	481.3	1,229.8	45
Hong Kong	2,274.0	7,909.7	234	3,089.1	9,450.8	9	815.1	1,541.1	37	827.8	1,573.1	38
Hungary	-413.8	-1,025.2	23	145.0	434.1	62	558.9	1,459.3	41	567.6	1,482.9	41
Iceland	-5.2	17.2	155	27.1	99.9	102	32.3	82.7	96	34.4	88.0	96
India	-2,303.4	-6,040.9	9	1,790.4	4,997.8	18	4,093.8	11,038.7	9	4,275.4	11,515.6	8
Indonesia	-1,015.6	-2,790.3	16	732.9	1,917.3	36	1,748.4	4,707.6	20	1,846.8	4,960.3	20
Iran	44.2	74.2	190	44.2	74.2	110	(-)	(-)	(X)	(-)	(-)	(X)
Iraq	-117.6	-521.6	35	166.4	632.2	54	284.0	1,153.8	46	293.8	1,183.9	48
Ireland	-2,326.7	-6,659.0	6	898.6	2,258.4	28	3,225.3	8,917.4	12	3,238.3	8,954.0	12
Israel	-1,242.9	-3,165.4	15	1,234.8	3,444.1	23	2,477.6	6,609.6	18	2,518.1	6,726.5	18
Italy	-2,275.1	-6,426.8	8	1,541.0	3,940.1	22	3,816.1	10,366.8	10	3,928.3	10,658.2	10
Jamaica	122.6	351.8	213	146.8	423.6	63	24.2	71.8	101	26.5	77.7	98
Japan	-7,124.7	-17,072.5	2	5,717.3	15,874.4	4	12,842.0	32,947.0	4	13,360.8	34,115.7	4
Jordan	-12.7	-34.3	67	107.3	307.3	71	120.0	341.6	69	123.2	349.9	69
Kazakhstan	31.6	18.4	157	40.7	158.7	90	9.0	140.4	87	9.3	147.5	87
Kenya	-14.6	22.1	161	34.1	162.2	89	48.7	140.1	88	50.7	145.9	88
Kiribati	1.0	3.4	130	1.1	3.9	183	0.1	0.6	186	0.1	0.7	186
Korea, North	0.0	0.2	105	0.0	0.2	221	(-)	(-)	(X)	(-)	(-)	(X)
Korea, South	-2,200.4	-6,920.4	5	4,062.2	10,690.2	7	6,262.6	17,610.6	6	6,476.3	18,206.5	6
Kosovo	-0.1	0.8	117	0.3	1.3	200	0.4	0.5	191	0.4	0.5	191
Kuwait	-55.9	-780.8	26	266.1	734.1	52	322.0	1,514.9	39	332.6	1,568.5	39
Kyrgyzstan	3.7	11.3	149	3.7	11.5	161	0.0	0.1	210	0.0	0.1	210
Laos	-2.4	-5.8	79	2.4	6.7	176	4.8	12.5	141	5.1	13.2	140
Latvia	-5.3	-0.1	94	24.8	70.4	113	30.1	70.5	103	31.7	74.0	102
Lebanon	74.6	334.2	212	78.3	349.1	69	3.7	14.9	138	3.9	15.5	138
Lesotho	-23.1	-62.7	57	0.0	0.2	224	23.2	62.8	104	23.8	64.8	104
Liberia	5.1	30.7	171	12.6	42.3	135	7.4	11.6	143	7.9	12.2	144
Libya	-8.5	-5.0	80	13.4	40.7	136	22.0	45.8	111	22.7	46.8	112
Liechtenstein	-20.5	-65.1	56	2.0	5.9	179	22.5	70.9	102	22.9	72.0	103
Lithuania	-72.0	-134.4	49	55.6	132.7	93	127.6	267.0	76	133.7	280.7	76
Luxembourg	180.9	240.5	204	243.0	417.7	64	62.1	177.3	79	63.9	181.2	79
Macau	57.7	106.6	192	65.7	126.5	97	8.0	19.9	124	8.2	20.5	126
Macedonia	-14.5	-52.1	63	1.4	3.1	188	15.9	55.2	107	16.2	56.4	107
Madagascar	-31.2	-57.4	60	6.9	18.9	151	38.1	76.3	98	38.5	77.4	100
Malawi	8.7	5.7	134	12.3	15.8	156	3.6	10.1	147	3.7	10.4	148

Exhibit 4. Exports, Imports, and Trade Balance by Country and Area, Not Seasonally Adjusted: 2015

In millions of dollars. Details may not equal totals due to rounding. (X) Not applicable. (-) Represents zero or less than one-half unit of measurement shown.

Country	Balance (Customs imports)			Exports Domestic & Foreign, F.A.S. basis			Imports Customs basis			Imports C.I.F. basis		
	March	Year-to-Date	Rank	March	Year-to-Date	Rank	March	Year-to-Date	Rank	March	Year-to-Date	Rank
Malaysia	-1,728.1	-4,678.9	11	1,166.6	3,049.2	24	2,894.8	7,728.1	14	2,964.8	7,902.9	14
Maldives	0.3	1.4	122	2.7	6.7	175	2.4	5.3	156	3.6	8.3	153
Mali	6.2	22.1	162	6.5	23.2	147	0.2	1.0	181	0.2	1.0	181
Malta	12.9	57.5	186	27.4	97.0	104	14.6	39.5	115	14.9	40.3	115
Marshall Islands	2.3	6.7	138	3.3	9.8	163	1.0	3.1	161	1.4	4.0	160
Martinique	10.6	34.7	174	10.8	46.2	127	0.2	11.6	144	0.2	12.4	143
Mauritania	10.9	23.0	164	11.0	23.3	146	0.1	0.3	201	0.1	0.3	201
Mauritius	-29.2	-81.6	52	2.3	6.4	177	31.5	88.0	94	32.4	90.3	94
Mayotte	0.2	1.2	121	0.2	1.2	201	(-)	0.0	217	(-)	0.0	218
Mexico	-5,499.8	-12,766.9	4	19,869.6	57,140.2	2	25,369.3	69,907.1	3	25,632.5	70,629.2	3
Micronesia	2.5	7.8	143	2.7	8.0	170	0.2	0.2	204	0.2	0.2	204
Moldova	-2.8	-7.2	78	1.3	3.2	186	4.0	10.4	146	4.3	11.0	146
Monaco	1.6	7.1	139	5.2	13.0	159	3.5	5.9	155	3.6	6.1	156
Mongolia	4.9	13.6	150	6.6	17.0	154	1.7	3.4	160	1.8	3.5	161
Montenegro	1.5	2.0	125	1.5	2.4	193	0.1	0.4	197	0.1	0.4	197
Montserrat	0.6	1.9	124	0.6	2.2	194	0.0	0.3	202	0.0	0.3	202
Morocco	55.5	251.4	207	159.0	523.5	58	103.5	272.1	75	107.3	292.0	73
Mozambique	7.0	16.3	154	13.6	42.7	134	6.5	26.4	121	6.6	26.6	122
Namibia	9.9	23.1	165	19.3	39.0	138	9.4	15.9	135	9.4	15.9	137
Nauru	0.4	0.4	109	0.4	0.5	211	0.0	0.1	212	0.0	0.1	213
Nepal	-4.9	-17.8	70	2.1	4.8	181	7.0	22.5	123	7.4	23.8	125
Netherlands	2,311.3	5,965.7	233	3,880.1	10,403.5	8	1,568.8	4,437.8	23	1,655.5	4,650.4	22
New Caledonia	0.7	6.6	137	7.0	19.2	150	6.3	12.6	140	6.5	13.1	141
New Zealand	-185.1	-371.1	41	290.4	769.0	50	475.5	1,140.1	48	495.0	1,186.7	47
Nicaragua	-169.4	-447.1	36	116.4	295.8	74	285.8	742.9	56	294.6	763.2	57
Niger	2.4	6.0	136	2.6	6.3	178	0.2	0.4	199	0.2	0.4	199
Nigeria	192.0	544.3	219	286.5	844.0	49	94.6	299.8	71	99.7	313.1	71
Niue	0.0	0.0	95	0.0	0.0	232	0.0	0.0	215	0.0	0.1	215
Norfolk Island	0.0	-1.1	87	0.0	0.0	231	(-)	1.1	178	(-)	1.2	180
Norway	7.0	-139.3	48	393.0	904.8	48	386.0	1,044.1	52	409.8	1,099.4	51
Oman	151.4	217.5	203	252.9	537.8	57	101.5	320.3	70	108.7	341.8	70
Pakistan	-124.2	-406.2	38	184.3	477.8	61	308.5	884.1	54	325.5	932.8	54
Palau	2.3	7.1	141	2.4	7.3	173	0.1	0.2	207	0.1	0.2	206
Panama	641.7	1,892.4	228	684.9	1,991.4	33	43.2	99.0	92	44.7	102.7	92
Papua New Guinea	5.9	45.1	180	12.0	63.5	121	6.1	18.5	126	6.3	19.1	129
Paraguay	96.9	373.8	215	107.5	414.3	65	10.6	40.5	114	11.1	43.4	114
Peru	381.7	916.7	224	766.7	2,216.3	29	385.0	1,299.6	42	405.0	1,378.4	42
Philippines	-342.6	-547.9	34	676.5	1,971.2	34	1,019.1	2,519.1	31	1,066.3	2,621.6	31
Pitcairn Islands	0.0	0.0	97	(-)	0.0	234	0.0	0.0	226	0.0	0.0	226
Poland	-55.7	-241.9	47	439.4	1,020.2	46	495.1	1,262.1	43	514.2	1,311.3	43
Portugal	-224.7	-442.7	37	86.4	294.7	75	311.1	737.4	57	322.8	764.9	56
Qatar	160.4	746.5	222	385.6	1,204.1	44	225.2	457.6	65	228.6	466.5	65
Reunion	0.3	-3.6	83	0.5	1.6	197	0.2	5.2	157	0.2	5.3	157
Romania	-100.5	-266.7	46	81.0	226.9	81	181.4	493.6	64	190.3	518.0	63
Russia	-867.0	-2,590.7	17	702.1	1,932.0	35	1,569.2	4,522.7	22	1,640.6	4,723.3	21
Rwanda	-2.4	-9.6	74	1.7	2.8	189	4.1	12.4	142	4.1	12.7	142
Samoa	2.3	7.1	140	2.6	7.7	171	0.3	0.6	189	0.3	0.6	187
San Marino	-0.3	-1.0	88	0.0	0.3	219	0.4	1.3	174	0.4	1.5	174
Sao Tome and Principe	0.3	0.4	108	0.4	0.5	213	0.0	0.1	211	0.0	0.1	211
Saudi Arabia	185.2	-721.2	29	1,747.7	4,545.3	19	1,562.5	5,266.5	19	1,657.7	5,552.6	19
Senegal	12.3	45.7	181	20.0	56.5	122	7.7	10.8	145	8.2	11.5	145
Serbia	-15.8	-60.8	59	10.3	26.9	143	26.1	87.7	95	26.6	89.2	95
Seychelles	0.6	2.3	127	1.2	3.8	184	0.6	1.5	173	0.6	1.5	173
Sierra Leone	7.6	22.8	163	8.2	24.4	144	0.7	1.5	172	0.7	1.6	172
Singapore	1,249.2	3,228.2	229	2,703.7	7,032.8	13	1,454.5	3,804.5	25	1,477.9	3,860.8	25
Sint Maarten	68.6	242.9	206	75.7	259.6	78	7.1	16.7	132	7.1	16.8	133
Slovakia	-214.1	-394.7	39	33.0	110.2	99	247.1	504.9	63	250.7	513.7	64
Slovenia	-38.5	-83.2	51	20.5	69.3	116	59.0	152.5	81	61.2	157.9	81
Solomon Islands	-0.4	-1.4	86	0.3	0.8	207	0.8	2.2	165	0.8	2.3	165
Somalia	2.2	8.1	144	2.3	8.4	168	0.1	0.3	203	0.1	0.3	203
South Africa	-118.9	-385.5	40	482.2	1,351.8	42	601.1	1,737.2	36	615.0	1,776.1	36
South Sudan	0.9	2.2	126	0.9	2.2	195	0.0	0.0	229	0.0	0.0	229
Spain	-462.3	-764.4	28	762.9	2,479.0	27	1,225.2	3,243.3	27	1,273.1	3,373.7	27
Sri Lanka	-253.4	-662.6	31	33.9	94.4	106	287.3	757.0	55	301.5	792.3	55
St Helena	0.7	0.8	118	0.7	1.4	199	0.0	0.6	188	0.0	0.6	189

Exhibit 4. Exports, Imports, and Trade Balance by Country and Area, Not Seasonally Adjusted: 2015

In millions of dollars. Details may not equal totals due to rounding. (X) Not applicable. (-) Represents zero or less than one-half unit of measurement shown.

Country	Balance (Customs imports)			Exports Domestic & Foreign, F.A.S. basis			Imports Customs basis			Imports C.I.F. basis		
	March	Year-to-Date	Rank	March	Year-to-Date	Rank	March	Year-to-Date	Rank	March	Year-to-Date	Rank
St Kitts and Nevis	7.1	19.3	159	12.5	37.8	139	5.4	18.0	128	5.5	18.5	130
St Lucia	8.4	87.0	191	12.3	93.3	107	3.9	6.3	154	4.1	6.6	155
St Pierre and Miquelon	0.0	0.0	100	0.0	0.0	228	0.0	0.0	228	0.0	0.0	228
St Vincent and the Grenadines	5.5	15.1	151	5.7	15.5	157	0.2	0.3	200	0.2	0.3	200
Sudan	-0.4	5.3	135	0.6	7.5	172	1.0	1.7	170	1.1	1.8	170
Suriname	24.4	44.1	178	35.9	102.2	100	11.5	58.1	105	12.4	62.5	105
Svalbard, Jan Mayen Island	0.2	0.2	104	0.2	0.2	222	0.0	0.0	225	0.0	0.0	225
Swaziland	1.4	4.4	132	1.7	5.3	180	0.3	0.9	182	0.3	0.9	182
Sweden	-519.5	-1,312.1	21	346.9	980.5	47	866.3	2,292.6	32	888.0	2,348.5	33
Switzerland	-373.1	-1,233.7	22	2,763.4	6,116.4	14	3,136.5	7,350.1	15	3,165.1	7,419.4	15
Syria	0.0	-0.3	91	0.3	0.8	205	0.3	1.2	177	0.4	1.2	177
Taiwan	-2,163.9	-4,329.2	12	1,958.8	5,682.5	16	4,122.7	10,011.8	11	4,290.8	10,402.7	11
Tajikistan	-8.8	-7.3	77	1.0	2.6	190	9.7	9.9	148	10.7	10.6	147
Tanzania	8.6	7.1	142	23.8	44.5	130	15.1	37.4	116	15.5	38.3	116
Thailand	-1,503.1	-3,799.0	13	1,114.7	2,947.2	25	2,617.7	6,746.2	16	2,717.1	6,987.5	16
Timor-Leste	0.2	0.3	107	0.3	0.4	216	0.0	0.1	214	0.0	0.1	214
Togo	2.1	15.7	152	3.1	18.3	152	1.0	2.7	164	1.0	2.8	164
Tokelau	-0.2	-0.3	92	0.0	0.2	225	0.2	0.4	193	0.2	0.5	193
Tonga	0.9	3.9	131	1.1	4.6	182	0.2	0.6	185	0.3	0.9	184
Trinidad and Tobago	-345.6	-864.2	24	205.4	602.5	55	551.0	1,466.7	40	576.4	1,550.1	40
Tunisia	-6.5	-9.3	75	40.3	134.9	92	46.8	144.2	85	48.4	148.1	86
Turkey	359.4	793.5	223	1,081.5	2,760.5	26	722.1	1,967.0	35	762.6	2,076.3	34
Turkmenistan	13.3	29.3	170	14.0	30.9	142	0.7	1.6	171	0.8	1.7	171
Turks and Caicos Islands	22.4	66.5	188	22.8	67.6	118	0.4	1.1	179	0.5	1.2	179
Tuvalu	0.0	0.0	98	0.0	0.0	230	0.0	0.0	221	0.0	0.0	220
Uganda	-11.0	-4.9	81	5.0	22.0	149	16.0	26.9	120	16.3	27.5	120
Ukraine	8.7	-2.7	84	71.3	232.1	80	62.6	234.9	77	66.1	248.4	77
United Arab Emirates	1,670.9	4,871.9	232	1,937.5	5,533.1	17	266.6	661.2	60	283.6	699.4	60
United Kingdom	-31.4	280.8	208	4,546.0	13,350.0	5	4,577.4	13,069.2	7	4,665.4	13,318.9	7
Uruguay	65.3	241.5	205	126.7	386.3	67	61.4	144.8	84	62.7	148.6	85
Uzbekistan	9.8	63.6	187	10.3	66.4	119	0.5	2.7	163	0.5	2.9	163
Vanuatu	2.1	1.5	123	2.2	2.5	191	0.1	1.1	180	0.1	1.2	178
Vatican City	0.3	0.9	119	0.3	1.0	203	0.1	0.1	209	0.1	0.2	209
Venezuela	-656.6	-2,073.6	18	792.6	2,092.6	31	1,449.2	4,166.2	24	1,510.3	4,324.0	24
Vietnam	-2,616.9	-6,607.3	7	598.0	1,631.2	38	3,214.9	8,238.5	13	3,369.9	8,628.8	13
Wallis and Futuna	0.0	0.1	103	0.0	0.1	226	(-)	(-)	(X)	(-)	(-)	(X)
West Bank Administered by Israel	-0.1	-1.0	89	0.1	0.2	223	0.2	1.2	176	0.2	1.3	176
Western Sahara	0.0	0.0	96	(-)	0.0	233	0.0	0.0	218	0.0	0.0	217
Yemen	31.2	24.0	167	31.4	71.0	112	0.2	47.0	110	0.2	47.7	111
Zambia	2.5	4.9	133	6.3	22.7	148	3.8	17.7	130	4.1	18.5	131
Zimbabwe	-3.9	-13.0	72	2.5	6.9	174	6.4	19.9	125	6.5	20.1	127
Unidentified (1)	(-)	(-)	(X)	(-)	(-)	(X)	(-)	(-)	(X)	(-)	(-)	(X)
Timing adjustment	(-)	-1,055.7	(X)	(-)	42.7	(X)	(-)	1,098.3	(X)	(-)	1,155.4	(X)

Exhibit 4. Exports, Imports, and Trade Balance by Country and Area, Not Seasonally Adjusted: 2015

In millions of dollars. Details may not equal totals due to rounding. (X) Not applicable. (-) Represents zero or less than one-half unit of measurement shown.

Country	Balance (Customs imports)			Exports Domestic & Foreign, F.A.S. basis			Imports Customs basis			Imports C.I.F. basis		
	March	Year-to-Date	Rank	March	Year-to-Date	Rank	March	Year-to-Date	Rank	March	Year-to-Date	Rank
Africa	132.7	447.8	(X)	2,190.4	6,406.8	(X)	2,057.6	5,959.0	(X)	2,131.7	6,184.6	(X)
APEC	-51,652.2	-133,258.2	(X)	81,996.0	229,923.4	(X)	133,648.2	363,181.5	(X)	138,077.2	374,839.9	(X)
ASEAN	-6,202.7	-15,779.3	(X)	7,054.2	18,737.9	(X)	13,256.9	34,517.2	(X)	13,763.2	35,767.1	(X)
Asia - South	-3,058.2	-8,296.9	(X)	2,188.3	5,948.1	(X)	5,246.5	14,245.0	(X)	5,481.4	14,867.2	(X)
Asia Near East	899.7	1,099.5	(X)	6,351.3	17,761.9	(X)	5,451.6	16,662.4	(X)	5,642.7	17,240.9	(X)
CAFTA-DR	322.0	1,252.6	(X)	2,491.8	7,019.9	(X)	2,169.9	5,767.2	(X)	2,280.7	6,055.0	(X)
Central American Common Market	114.3	552.8	(X)	1,867.4	5,275.8	(X)	1,753.0	4,723.0	(X)	1,852.8	4,983.1	(X)
Euro Area	-10,638.1	-26,566.4	(X)	18,202.9	51,492.6	(X)	28,841.1	78,058.9	(X)	29,502.0	79,787.3	(X)
Europe	-13,389.8	-34,222.9	(X)	29,569.3	81,788.8	(X)	42,959.1	116,011.8	(X)	43,975.6	118,701.0	(X)
European Union	-12,669.5	-31,326.3	(X)	24,188.3	68,723.1	(X)	36,857.8	100,049.4	(X)	37,694.1	102,254.7	(X)
LAFTA	-4,198.6	-9,412.7	(X)	28,873.1	82,829.5	(X)	33,071.7	92,242.2	(X)	33,734.3	94,082.6	(X)
NATO Allies	-9,162.1	-26,383.6	(X)	49,033.8	135,932.7	(X)	58,195.9	162,316.3	(X)	59,646.5	166,361.6	(X)
NICs	-841.1	-111.7	(X)	11,813.8	32,856.3	(X)	12,654.9	32,968.0	(X)	13,072.7	34,043.1	(X)
North America	-6,262.1	-17,879.2	(X)	44,904.1	126,487.2	(X)	51,166.2	144,366.4	(X)	52,052.5	146,959.8	(X)
OECD	-26,967.4	-70,250.1	(X)	85,253.8	237,476.5	(X)	112,221.2	307,726.6	(X)	114,791.6	314,590.1	(X)
OPEC	1,153.8	750.5	(X)	6,407.3	17,853.6	(X)	5,253.4	17,103.1	(X)	5,510.1	17,890.7	(X)
Pacific Rim Countries	-41,150.3	-104,450.7	(X)	32,536.7	90,743.9	(X)	73,687.0	195,194.5	(X)	76,769.9	203,063.2	(X)
South/Central America	3,008.8	8,540.8	(X)	13,767.5	39,032.1	(X)	10,758.7	30,491.2	(X)	11,305.3	32,011.3	(X)
Twenty Latin American Republics	-3,173.5	-6,137.3	(X)	32,191.6	92,170.6	(X)	35,365.1	98,307.9	(X)	36,141.7	100,443.7	(X)

Africa - Algeria, Angola, Benin, Botswana, British Indian Ocean Territories, Burkina Faso, Burundi, Cameroon, Cabo Verde, Central African Republic, Chad, Comoros, Congo (Brazzaville), Congo (Kinshasa), Cote d'Ivoire, Djibouti, Egypt, Equatorial Guinea, Eritrea, Ethiopia, French Southern and Antarctic Lands, Gabon, Gambia, Ghana, Guinea, Guinea-Bissau, Kenya, Lesotho, Liberia, Libya, Madagascar, Malawi, Mali, Mauritania, Mauritius, Mayotte, Morocco, Mozambique, Namibia, Niger, Nigeria, Reunion, Rwanda, Sao Tome and Principe, Senegal, Seychelles, Sierra Leone, Somalia, South Africa, South Sudan, St. Helena, Sudan, Swaziland, Tanzania, Togo, Tunisia, Uganda, Western Sahara, Zambia, Zimbabwe.

APEC (Asia - Pacific Economic Cooperation) - Australia, Brunei, Canada, Chile, China, Hong Kong, Indonesia, Japan, Korea (South), Malaysia, Mexico, New Zealand, Papua New Guinea, Peru, Philippines, Russia, Singapore, Taiwan, Thailand, Vietnam.

ASEAN (Association of Southeast Asian Nations) - Brunei, Burma, Cambodia, Indonesia, Laos, Malaysia, Philippines, Singapore, Thailand, Vietnam.

Asia - South - Afghanistan, Bangladesh, India, Nepal, Pakistan, Sri Lanka.

Asia Near East - Bahrain, Gaza Strip Administered by Israel, Iran, Iraq, Israel, Jordan, Kuwait, Lebanon, Oman, Qatar, Saudi Arabia, Syria, United Arab Emirates, West Bank Administered by Israel, Yemen.

CAFTA-DR (Dominican Republic-Central America-United States Free Trade Agreement) - Costa Rica, Dominican Republic, El Salvador, Guatemala, Honduras, Nicaragua.

Central American Common Market - Costa Rica, El Salvador, Guatemala, Honduras, Nicaragua.

Euro Area - Austria, Belgium, Cyprus, Estonia, Finland, France, Germany, Greece, Ireland, Italy, Latvia, Lithuania, Luxembourg, Malta, Netherlands, Portugal, Slovakia, Slovenia, Spain.

Europe - Albania, Andorra, Armenia, Austria, Azerbaijan, Belarus, Belgium, Bosnia-Herzegovina, Bulgaria, Croatia, Cyprus, Czech Republic, Denmark, Estonia, Faroe Islands, Finland, France, Georgia, Germany, Gibraltar, Greece, Hungary, Iceland, Ireland, Italy, Kazakhstan, Kosovo, Kyrgyzstan, Latvia, Liechtenstein, Lithuania, Luxembourg, Macedonia, Malta, Moldova, Monaco, Montenegro, Netherlands, Norway, Poland, Portugal, Romania, Russia, San Marino, Serbia, Slovakia, Slovenia, Spain, Svalbard, Jan Mayen Island, Sweden, Switzerland, Tajikistan, Turkey, Turkmenistan, Ukraine, United Kingdom, Uzbekistan, Vatican City.

European Union - Austria, Belgium, Bulgaria, Croatia, Cyprus, Czech Republic, Denmark, Estonia, Finland, France, Germany, Greece, Hungary, Ireland, Italy, Latvia, Lithuania, Luxembourg, Malta, Netherlands, Poland, Portugal, Romania, Slovakia, Slovenia, Spain, Sweden, United Kingdom.

LAFTA (Latin American Free Trade Area) - Argentina, Bolivia, Brazil, Chile, Colombia, Ecuador, Mexico, Paraguay, Peru, Uruguay, Venezuela.

NATO (North Atlantic Treaty Organization) Allies - Belgium, Bulgaria, Canada, Czech Republic, Denmark, Estonia, France, Germany, Greece, Hungary, Iceland, Italy, Latvia, Lithuania, Luxembourg, Netherlands, Norway, Poland, Portugal, Romania, Slovakia, Slovenia, Spain, Turkey, United Kingdom.

NICs (Newly Industrialized Countries) - Hong Kong, Korea (South), Singapore, Taiwan.

North America - Canada, Mexico.

OECD (Organization for Economic Cooperation and Development) - Australia, Austria, Belgium, Canada, Chile, Czech Republic, Denmark, Estonia, Finland, France, Germany, Greece, Hungary, Iceland, Ireland, Israel, Italy, Japan, Korea (South), Luxembourg, Mexico, Netherlands, New Zealand, Norway, Poland, Portugal, Slovakia, Slovenia, Spain, Sweden, Switzerland, Turkey, United Kingdom.

OPEC (Organization of the Petroleum Exporting Countries) - Algeria, Angola, Ecuador, Iran, Iraq, Kuwait, Libya, Nigeria, Qatar, Saudi Arabia, United Arab Emirates, Venezuela.

Pacific Rim Countries - Australia, Brunei, China, Hong Kong, Indonesia, Japan, Korea (South), Macau, Malaysia, New Zealand, Papua New Guinea, Philippines, Singapore, Taiwan.

South/Central America - Anguilla, Antigua and Barbuda, Argentina, Aruba, Bahamas, Barbados, Belize, Bermuda, Bolivia, Brazil, British Virgin Islands, Cayman Islands, Chile, Colombia, Costa Rica, Cuba, Curacao, Dominica, Dominican Republic, Ecuador, El Salvador, Falkland Islands (Islas Malvinas), French Guiana, Grenada, Guadeloupe, Guatemala, Guyana, Haiti, Honduras, Jamaica, Martinique, Montserrat, Nicaragua, Panama, Paraguay, Peru, St. Kitts and Nevis, Sint Maarten, St. Lucia, St. Vincent and the Grenadines, Suriname, Trinidad and Tobago, Turks and Caicos Islands, Uruguay, Venezuela.

Twenty Latin American Republics - Argentina, Bolivia, Brazil, Chile, Colombia, Costa Rica, Cuba, Dominican Republic, Ecuador, El Salvador, Guatemala, Haiti, Honduras, Mexico, Nicaragua, Panama, Paraguay, Peru, Uruguay, Venezuela.

(1) The export totals reflect shipments of certain grains, oilseeds, and satellites that are not included in the country/area totals.

NOTE: Country grouping data reflect the groups as they were at the time of reporting.

Exhibit 4a. Exports, Imports and Trade Balance by Country and Area, Not Seasonally Adjusted: 2014

In millions of dollars. Details may not equal totals due to rounding. (X) Not applicable. (-) Represents zero or less than one-half unit of measurement shown.

Country	Balance (Customs imports)			Exports (Domestic & Foreign, F.A.S. basis)			Imports Customs basis			Imports C.I.F. basis		
	March	Year-to-Date	Rank	March	Year-to-Date	Rank	March	Year-to-Date	Rank	March	Year-to-Date	Rank
TOTAL	-51,441.3	-154,571.6	(X)	141,905.2	393,141.3	(X)	193,346.4	547,712.9	(X)	198,672.8	563,015.8	(X)
Afghanistan	64.8	221.8	207	92.2	253.5	76	27.4	31.7	115	27.5	32.0	117
Albania	2.3	4.5	133	4.8	11.9	167	2.5	7.4	147	2.6	7.8	148
Algeria	-112.4	-194.0	51	207.5	787.0	54	319.9	981.0	53	332.2	1,012.9	53
Andorra	0.2	0.9	114	0.2	1.0	206	0.0	0.1	209	0.0	0.1	211
Angola	-235.2	-785.5	28	121.8	402.4	70	357.0	1,187.9	46	364.1	1,210.9	47
Anguilla	3.0	8.0	142	3.5	9.2	172	0.5	1.2	181	0.6	1.3	182
Antigua and Barbuda	7.0	37.8	175	10.7	42.1	133	3.7	4.3	162	3.7	4.3	162
Argentina	437.1	1,711.5	226	849.9	2,629.0	28	412.8	917.5	55	434.5	960.2	55
Armenia	-3.1	-6.8	78	5.6	13.5	164	8.7	20.3	126	9.1	21.4	126
Aruba	136.8	280.7	209	138.5	286.5	74	1.7	5.9	153	1.7	6.0	154
Australia	1,342.8	4,132.7	229	2,132.9	6,382.5	15	790.1	2,249.8	35	814.1	2,313.3	35
Austria	-773.8	-1,326.6	23	203.9	1,134.3	47	977.7	2,460.9	33	1,000.1	2,517.6	33
Azerbaijan	-86.5	-36.7	69	28.8	79.0	116	115.2	115.7	89	117.9	113.4	90
Bahamas	353.0	886.2	219	410.5	1,057.8	48	57.5	171.6	82	61.1	180.6	82
Bahrain	26.5	-38.1	68	96.7	240.4	79	70.3	278.5	74	73.7	289.3	74
Bangladesh	-235.4	-891.6	26	245.0	545.1	60	480.5	1,436.7	43	499.2	1,492.0	44
Barbados	43.9	109.2	188	46.9	119.9	103	3.0	10.7	143	3.2	11.3	142
Belarus	-1.4	-6.4	79	6.7	19.2	153	8.1	25.5	123	8.6	27.5	121
Belgium	1,235.8	3,578.7	228	3,073.1	8,302.3	11	1,837.3	4,723.7	25	1,885.2	4,840.7	25
Belize	9.4	27.4	166	22.5	53.5	125	13.1	26.2	120	13.7	27.4	122
Benin	88.5	203.5	203	89.3	205.5	88	0.7	2.0	171	0.8	2.1	171
Bermuda	75.3	140.5	196	76.3	143.5	97	1.0	3.0	165	1.0	3.1	166
Bhutan	0.2	0.2	104	0.2	0.3	218	0.0	0.1	210	0.0	0.1	209
Bolivia	-115.0	-264.6	48	85.0	234.3	80	199.9	498.9	66	200.8	501.2	66
Bosnia and Herzegovina	-4.9	-13.8	73	2.2	6.0	186	7.1	19.8	128	7.3	20.4	129
Botswana	-24.0	-47.4	61	3.2	6.7	183	27.2	54.0	104	27.8	55.1	105
Brazil	1,836.6	4,281.7	231	3,943.3	10,745.3	9	2,106.7	6,463.6	18	2,183.0	6,708.6	18
British Indian Ocean Territories	-0.4	-4.3	83	0.1	0.1	226	0.5	4.4	161	0.5	4.4	161
British Virgin Islands	21.2	73.0	185	21.3	73.8	119	0.2	0.8	186	0.2	0.8	185
Brunei	181.3	197.7	202	184.0	203.4	89	2.7	5.7	155	2.7	5.8	155
Bulgaria	-12.6	-38.2	67	34.9	101.5	107	47.6	139.7	84	50.4	146.1	84
Burkina Faso	2.1	15.1	151	2.2	15.5	160	0.1	0.4	194	0.1	0.4	194
Burma	5.3	5.2	134	11.4	25.0	145	6.1	19.8	127	6.3	20.4	127
Burundi	0.3	-1.4	87	0.5	1.1	203	0.2	2.4	169	0.2	2.5	170
Cabo Verde	0.5	1.2	118	0.5	1.4	202	0.1	0.2	197	0.1	0.2	197
Cambodia	-271.1	-697.5	32	23.4	73.7	120	294.5	771.2	58	304.8	798.7	58
Cameroon	-24.5	-4.8	82	18.6	52.0	126	43.0	56.9	103	46.5	61.4	103
Canada	-2,278.2	-8,473.2	6	27,147.6	73,060.8	1	29,425.8	81,533.9	2	30,063.9	83,344.5	2
Cayman Islands	45.5	156.2	199	48.2	161.6	94	2.6	5.4	157	2.7	5.6	157
Central African Republic	0.7	1.2	119	0.7	1.4	201	0.0	0.2	196	0.0	0.2	196
Chad	-143.6	-432.2	41	3.3	10.4	170	146.8	442.6	69	149.7	451.9	69
Chile	469.3	1,373.6	225	1,453.8	3,979.4	22	984.5	2,605.8	32	1,081.7	2,872.3	30
China	-20,403.5	-69,104.8	1	10,830.2	31,066.1	3	31,233.7	100,170.8	1	32,546.7	104,419.9	1
Christmas Island	0.0	0.3	107	0.0	0.4	215	0.0	0.1	214	0.0	0.1	212
Cocos (Keeling) Islands	-0.1	0.4	109	0.0	0.6	212	0.1	0.2	199	0.1	0.2	198
Colombia	44.9	-196.0	50	1,745.9	4,863.8	18	1,701.0	5,059.8	23	1,747.9	5,214.8	23
Comoros	0.0	0.1	101	0.0	0.2	220	0.0	0.1	204	0.0	0.1	204
Congo (Brazzaville)	4.9	-44.5	62	14.3	39.5	136	9.4	84.0	95	9.6	85.0	95
Congo (Kinshasa)	9.1	0.3	106	10.4	31.4	142	1.3	31.2	118	1.3	31.6	119
Cook Islands	0.3	0.9	115	0.3	1.0	205	0.0	0.1	206	0.0	0.1	207
Costa Rica	-328.4	-732.0	30	728.9	1,996.2	34	1,057.3	2,728.2	31	1,081.6	2,797.5	32
Cote d'Ivoire	-221.1	-522.9	37	12.6	42.9	132	233.6	565.8	64	244.0	587.0	64
Croatia	6.4	7.1	140	50.4	122.4	102	43.9	115.3	90	45.1	118.6	89
Cuba	53.6	133.2	195	53.6	133.2	100	(-)	(-)	(X)	(-)	(-)	(X)
Curaçao	12.2	100.6	187	33.0	148.6	96	20.8	48.0	107	21.0	48.4	109
Cyprus	5.1	24.2	165	13.6	43.2	130	8.5	19.0	131	8.7	19.3	131
Czech Republic	-176.7	-430.9	42	175.4	532.0	61	352.2	962.9	54	363.2	992.0	54
Denmark	-477.7	-1,364.3	22	219.8	557.1	58	697.5	1,921.4	37	709.1	1,952.6	37
Djibouti	6.3	22.9	163	6.8	23.6	149	0.5	0.8	185	0.5	0.8	186
Dominica	4.7	13.8	149	5.1	14.4	163	0.4	0.6	190	0.4	0.7	190
Dominican Republic	321.4	886.5	220	706.9	1,891.7	36	385.5	1,005.2	51	397.2	1,033.3	52
Ecuador	-234.7	-1,096.7	25	614.1	1,792.1	38	848.8	2,888.9	29	881.4	3,009.6	29
Egypt	577.4	1,259.3	224	703.8	1,607.3	39	126.3	348.0	71	132.6	364.9	71
El Salvador	95.5	281.9	210	309.5	818.0	52	213.9	536.1	65	220.7	553.6	65
Equatorial Guinea	19.0	72.5	184	19.6	116.2	105	0.6	43.7	109	0.6	44.7	110
Eritrea	0.2	0.5	110	0.2	0.6	213	0.0	0.1	213	0.0	0.1	215

Exhibit 4a. Exports, Imports and Trade Balance by Country and Area, Not Seasonally Adjusted: 2014

In millions of dollars. Details may not equal totals due to rounding. (X) Not applicable. (-) Represents zero or less than one-half unit of measurement shown.

Country	Balance (Customs imports)			Exports Domestic & Foreign, F.A.S. basis			Imports Customs basis			Imports C.I.F. basis		
	March	Year-to-Date	Rank	March	Year-to-Date	Rank	March	Year-to-Date	Rank	March	Year-to-Date	Rank
Estonia	-19.8	-41.8	64	33.7	77.2	118	53.4	119.0	88	54.5	121.7	88
Ethiopia	-6.3	204.1	204	18.1	251.0	77	24.3	47.0	108	25.1	48.6	108
Falkland Islands (Islas Malvinas)	-4.4	1.8	123	0.0	6.8	182	4.4	5.0	159	4.5	5.0	160
Faroe Islands	-14.9	-40.0	66	0.4	0.6	210	15.3	40.6	110	20.7	54.2	106
Fiji	-1.7	-11.8	74	12.0	19.8	152	13.7	31.6	116	16.5	37.8	114
Finland	-277.1	-522.9	36	198.3	555.3	59	475.4	1,078.3	49	491.4	1,122.6	49
France	-1,650.0	-3,967.7	13	2,597.9	7,494.3	13	4,247.9	11,462.0	9	4,317.6	11,643.1	9
French Guiana	0.7	7.4	141	0.7	7.4	179	0.0	0.0	225	0.0	0.0	225
French Polynesia	5.3	22.6	162	13.0	34.4	140	7.8	11.8	140	8.0	12.4	140
French Southern and Antarctic Lands	0.1	0.3	105	0.1	0.3	219	0.0	0.0	228	0.0	0.0	228
Gabon	-60.3	-182.4	52	22.0	61.0	123	82.2	243.4	76	87.6	256.6	76
Gambia	4.4	10.7	145	4.5	10.8	169	0.1	0.1	207	0.1	0.1	206
Gaza Strip Administered by Israel	0.0	0.0	93	(-)	(-)	(X)	0.0	0.0	216	0.1	0.1	216
Georgia	33.3	122.7	192	53.4	160.8	95	20.0	38.2	113	20.9	39.8	112
Germany	-5,908.8	-15,646.4	3	4,658.8	12,883.1	5	10,567.6	28,529.4	5	10,769.0	29,051.1	5
Ghana	76.3	142.7	197	99.5	214.6	83	23.2	72.0	99	24.5	75.8	99
Gibraltar	271.7	1,041.8	222	271.7	1,041.9	50	0.1	0.1	215	0.1	0.1	214
Greece	-13.0	-44.2	63	69.8	188.7	92	82.8	232.9	77	88.1	248.5	77
Greenland	7.4	6.4	139	7.9	8.1	176	0.5	1.7	177	0.5	1.7	178
Grenada	9.6	19.3	158	10.8	21.7	150	1.2	2.4	170	1.3	2.6	169
Guadeloupe	35.8	115.8	190	36.0	116.8	104	0.2	1.0	183	0.2	1.1	183
Guatemala	105.1	490.1	217	465.8	1,482.4	43	360.7	992.4	52	396.2	1,076.6	51
Guinea	-3.4	-11.0	75	9.0	14.6	162	12.4	25.6	122	16.7	35.2	115
Guinea-Bissau	0.1	0.4	108	0.1	0.4	214	(-)	0.0	218	(-)	0.0	218
Guyana	-9.5	-18.5	72	30.0	77.5	117	39.5	96.0	91	43.0	100.8	91
Haiti	61.2	121.6	191	128.3	305.8	73	67.2	184.1	81	68.5	187.6	81
Heard and McDonald Islands	1.0	1.0	116	1.0	1.0	204	0.0	0.0	219	0.0	0.0	219
Honduras	228.6	457.1	216	620.1	1,489.9	41	391.5	1,032.8	50	413.7	1,095.6	50
Hong Kong	2,373.0	9,234.9	234	3,305.7	10,849.8	8	932.6	1,615.0	40	943.2	1,642.6	41
Hungary	-234.9	-614.3	34	207.6	494.3	63	442.5	1,108.6	48	449.2	1,127.4	48
Iceland	27.6	34.5	173	54.6	112.3	106	27.1	77.8	96	28.9	83.2	96
India	-2,168.0	-5,937.1	7	1,714.2	4,663.6	19	3,882.2	10,600.6	10	4,021.8	10,989.3	10
Indonesia	-1,125.9	-2,831.6	18	684.6	2,052.1	33	1,810.5	4,883.7	24	1,894.5	5,111.2	24
Iran	18.8	43.0	177	18.8	43.0	131	(-)	(-)	(X)	(-)	(-)	(X)
Iraq	-728.4	-2,288.8	20	203.1	448.8	67	931.4	2,737.6	30	956.5	2,802.2	31
Ireland	-1,812.4	-5,420.7	9	735.9	1,829.8	37	2,548.3	7,250.5	15	2,560.4	7,281.7	15
Israel	-207.1	-1,803.9	21	1,408.6	3,631.9	23	1,615.7	5,435.7	21	1,653.5	5,551.7	21
Italy	-1,706.7	-5,040.6	11	1,851.1	4,429.9	20	3,557.8	9,470.4	11	3,665.1	9,750.9	11
Jamaica	159.8	429.4	215	186.4	500.6	62	26.6	71.2	101	29.8	78.1	98
Japan	-5,941.7	-16,526.3	2	6,026.1	16,900.2	4	11,967.8	33,426.4	4	12,262.1	34,252.6	4
Jordan	39.5	31.4	170	137.3	334.3	72	97.7	302.9	73	99.9	309.5	73
Kazakhstan	-7.3	-173.9	53	57.9	205.8	87	65.1	379.8	70	68.9	393.1	70
Kenya	-6.5	-22.6	71	38.0	99.2	108	44.5	121.8	86	45.8	125.8	86
Kiribati	0.0	0.9	113	0.4	1.6	199	0.4	0.7	188	0.4	0.8	187
Korea, North	10.1	11.2	146	10.1	11.2	168	(-)	(-)	(X)	(-)	(-)	(X)
Korea, South	-1,255.9	-4,174.4	12	4,363.6	11,356.6	7	5,619.5	15,531.0	6	5,794.7	16,030.4	6
Kosovo	2.2	3.0	128	2.2	3.1	194	0.0	0.1	202	0.0	0.1	202
Kuwait	-635.4	-2,758.3	19	223.7	815.8	53	859.1	3,574.1	26	884.1	3,667.3	26
Kyrgyzstan	7.2	15.1	150	7.2	15.7	159	0.1	0.6	191	0.1	0.6	191
Laos	0.2	1.8	122	2.0	7.0	181	1.8	5.2	158	1.9	5.5	159
Latvia	38.7	90.6	186	62.0	143.4	98	23.4	52.8	105	24.3	55.4	104
Lebanon	67.2	196.1	201	74.1	213.7	84	6.9	17.6	132	7.3	18.5	132
Lesotho	-34.9	-119.4	56	0.0	0.9	207	35.0	120.4	87	35.8	125.7	87
Liberia	18.9	31.4	171	25.1	47.8	129	6.2	16.4	134	6.4	17.0	133
Libya	43.2	112.4	189	49.3	122.4	101	6.1	10.0	144	6.2	10.1	144
Liechtenstein	-25.2	-64.7	59	2.3	7.2	180	27.5	71.9	100	27.9	72.9	101
Lithuania	-30.7	-123.5	55	100.1	210.9	85	130.8	334.4	72	134.2	346.1	72
Luxembourg	50.9	331.6	211	107.3	457.5	64	56.4	125.9	85	58.5	130.9	85
Macau	31.9	66.7	182	36.3	82.7	112	4.5	15.9	135	4.6	16.4	135
Macedonia	-12.4	-30.6	70	2.7	8.0	177	15.1	38.6	112	15.4	39.5	113
Madagascar	-13.7	-40.6	65	2.9	9.0	173	16.6	49.5	106	17.0	50.8	107
Malawi	-1.4	12.8	148	3.2	24.8	146	4.7	11.9	139	4.9	12.7	138

Exhibit 4a. Exports, Imports and Trade Balance by Country and Area, Not Seasonally Adjusted: 2014

In millions of dollars. Details may not equal totals due to rounding. (X) Not applicable. (-) Represents zero or less than one-half unit of measurement shown.

Country	Balance (Customs imports)			Exports Domestic & Foreign, F.A.S. basis			Imports Customs basis			Imports C.I.F. basis		
	March	Year-to-Date	Rank	March	Year-to-Date	Rank	March	Year-to-Date	Rank	March	Year-to-Date	Rank
Malaysia	-1,214.0	-3,515.4	14	1,181.2	3,047.3	24	2,395.2	6,562.7	17	2,457.4	6,732.9	17
Maldives	1.6	2.1	125	3.5	7.9	178	1.8	5.8	154	2.7	8.6	147
Mali	13.0	16.6	154	13.1	17.0	157	0.1	0.4	192	0.1	0.4	193
Malta	104.2	129.5	194	120.5	168.8	93	16.2	39.3	111	16.6	40.2	111
Marshall Islands	1.6	5.5	135	2.6	10.2	171	1.0	4.7	160	1.2	5.5	158
Martinique	10.8	42.8	176	17.4	68.2	121	6.7	25.5	124	6.8	26.0	124
Mauritania	6.0	-5.0	81	6.5	26.4	143	0.4	31.4	117	0.4	31.7	118
Mauritius	-26.6	-81.7	58	3.1	6.7	184	29.6	88.4	93	30.4	90.7	93
Mayotte	0.6	2.2	126	0.6	2.2	196	(-)	(-)	(X)	(-)	(-)	(X)
Mexico	-5,058.7	-11,787.5	4	19,896.9	57,392.0	2	24,955.6	69,179.5	3	25,201.6	69,915.2	3
Micronesia	2.8	8.7	143	2.9	8.8	174	0.1	0.1	203	0.1	0.1	203
Moldova	0.2	1.4	120	2.7	8.7	175	2.5	7.3	148	2.7	7.7	149
Monaco	1.0	9.5	144	3.0	16.1	158	2.1	6.5	151	2.1	6.6	152
Mongolia	15.6	37.3	174	15.9	38.1	137	0.3	0.8	184	0.3	0.9	184
Montenegro	1.2	3.1	129	1.3	3.8	190	0.1	0.7	187	0.1	0.7	188
Montserrat	1.1	1.7	121	1.1	1.9	198	0.1	0.1	200	0.1	0.2	200
Morocco	95.4	406.4	213	180.2	621.9	56	84.8	215.5	78	90.1	229.8	78
Mozambique	42.5	62.2	180	48.8	81.8	113	6.3	19.7	130	6.4	19.9	130
Namibia	10.6	18.7	157	20.1	86.3	111	9.5	67.6	102	9.6	67.8	102
Nauru	0.0	0.0	94	0.0	0.1	228	0.0	0.1	208	0.0	0.1	208
Nepal	-5.1	-8.4	76	3.0	13.0	165	8.1	21.4	125	8.6	22.8	125
Netherlands	1,770.5	5,127.5	233	3,727.4	10,216.9	10	1,956.9	5,089.4	22	2,059.9	5,287.2	22
New Caledonia	14.5	32.1	172	23.9	51.8	127	9.3	19.7	129	9.6	20.4	128
New Zealand	-24.8	-147.1	54	307.0	755.0	55	331.9	902.1	56	347.7	946.1	56
Nicaragua	-156.4	-458.1	40	87.7	222.6	81	244.1	680.7	60	250.9	701.5	61
Niger	3.7	11.6	147	4.0	12.3	166	0.3	0.7	189	0.3	0.7	189
Nigeria	-182.2	52.9	179	452.8	1,338.2	44	634.9	1,285.3	45	650.0	1,315.6	45
Niue	0.0	-0.1	92	0.0	0.0	229	0.0	0.1	211	0.0	0.1	213
Norfolk Island	0.0	0.7	112	(-)	0.7	209	0.0	0.0	226	0.0	0.0	226
Norway	-342.7	-287.0	46	371.4	1,294.6	45	714.1	1,581.6	42	738.6	1,635.5	42
Oman	50.9	151.3	198	176.5	408.1	69	125.5	256.9	75	134.1	275.3	75
Pakistan	-170.7	-521.5	38	122.2	378.1	71	292.9	899.6	57	308.3	946.1	57
Palau	1.9	5.5	136	1.9	5.6	187	0.0	0.1	212	0.0	0.1	210
Panama	1,008.7	2,496.3	227	1,033.4	2,581.1	29	24.7	84.7	94	26.2	88.4	94
Papua New Guinea	1.0	3.3	130	10.1	32.2	141	9.1	28.9	119	9.4	29.7	120
Paraguay	147.4	424.8	214	158.2	457.3	65	10.8	32.5	114	11.4	34.4	116
Peru	302.5	965.3	221	749.2	2,567.0	30	446.8	1,601.7	41	465.4	1,678.9	40
Philippines	-86.3	-196.4	49	798.8	2,169.9	32	885.1	2,366.3	34	915.2	2,445.5	34
Pitcairn Islands	(-)	0.0	97	(-)	(-)	(X)	(-)	0.0	229	(-)	0.0	229
Poland	-114.1	-307.2	45	332.4	879.3	51	446.5	1,186.5	47	461.8	1,225.0	46
Portugal	-203.1	-482.2	39	101.2	282.6	75	304.3	764.8	59	313.8	791.7	59
Qatar	376.1	583.9	218	656.9	1,202.8	46	280.8	618.9	63	286.2	632.3	63
Reunion	-1.6	-5.1	80	0.4	2.2	197	2.1	7.3	149	2.1	7.4	150
Romania	-100.5	-274.4	47	93.4	202.5	90	193.9	476.9	68	202.5	495.2	68
Russia	-1,535.0	-3,481.1	15	1,012.8	2,831.8	26	2,547.7	6,312.9	19	2,641.3	6,526.8	19
Rwanda	0.1	-1.1	89	0.6	5.2	189	0.5	6.2	152	0.5	6.5	153
Samoa	2.3	4.0	132	2.4	5.2	188	0.2	1.2	182	0.2	1.4	181
San Marino	-0.5	-1.4	86	0.1	0.2	221	0.7	1.6	178	0.8	1.9	174
Sao Tome and Principe	0.0	0.0	98	(-)	0.1	227	0.0	0.0	217	0.0	0.0	217
Saudi Arabia	-3,250.1	-10,350.2	5	1,631.8	4,099.5	21	4,881.9	14,449.7	7	5,014.6	14,849.8	7
Senegal	11.3	45.3	178	13.5	50.8	128	2.2	5.5	156	2.3	5.7	156
Serbia	-11.9	-48.5	60	8.2	24.5	147	20.1	73.0	98	20.5	74.2	100
Seychelles	-0.3	1.8	124	1.3	3.7	192	1.5	1.9	172	1.6	2.0	173
Sierra Leone	-1.5	6.0	137	9.1	18.5	154	10.6	12.6	138	10.7	12.6	139
Singapore	1,334.6	4,177.8	230	2,589.6	7,734.4	12	1,255.0	3,556.7	27	1,274.7	3,609.2	27
Sint Maarten	64.1	230.7	208	68.2	247.3	78	4.1	16.6	133	4.1	16.7	134
Slovakia	-140.2	-395.3	43	36.5	92.8	110	176.7	488.1	67	180.1	496.5	67
Slovenia	-46.5	-116.0	57	13.8	40.6	134	60.3	156.6	83	62.3	161.8	83
Solomon Islands	0.1	-1.5	84	0.5	1.4	200	0.4	2.9	166	0.5	3.3	165
Somalia	16.6	17.7	155	16.7	17.9	155	0.0	0.1	201	0.0	0.1	201
South Africa	-95.2	-379.8	44	576.4	1,534.9	40	671.6	1,914.6	38	685.2	1,951.4	38
South Sudan	1.6	2.3	127	1.6	2.3	195	(-)	0.0	227	(-)	0.0	227
Spain	-407.8	-638.1	33	809.9	2,533.9	31	1,217.7	3,172.0	28	1,256.1	3,273.4	28
Sri Lanka	-222.1	-598.2	35	22.2	79.8	115	244.3	678.0	61	255.6	708.8	60
St Helena	0.3	-1.4	85	0.3	0.3	217	0.0	1.7	175	0.0	1.8	177

Exhibit 4a. Exports, Imports and Trade Balance by Country and Area, Not Seasonally Adjusted: 2014

In millions of dollars. Details may not equal totals due to rounding. (X) Not applicable. (-) Represents zero or less than one-half unit of measurement shown.

Country	Balance (Customs imports)			Exports Domestic & Foreign, F.A.S. basis			Imports Customs basis			Imports C.I.F. basis		
	March	Year-to-Date	Rank	March	Year-to-Date	Rank	March	Year-to-Date	Rank	March	Year-to-Date	Rank
St Kitts and Nevis	6.4	22.2	161	11.3	35.2	138	4.9	13.0	137	5.1	13.4	137
St Lucia	18.3	126.6	193	21.7	133.3	99	3.4	6.7	150	3.5	7.0	151
St Pierre and Miquelon	(-)	0.0	96	(-)	(-)	(X)	(-)	0.0	224	(-)	0.0	224
St Vincent and the Grenadines	7.1	20.9	160	7.2	21.2	151	0.1	0.3	195	0.1	0.3	195
Sudan	19.0	23.9	164	19.7	25.6	144	0.7	1.7	176	0.8	1.9	176
Suriname	19.6	20.7	159	37.6	97.9	109	18.0	77.3	97	19.2	83.1	97
Svalbard, Jan Mayen Island	0.6	0.6	111	0.6	0.6	211	(-)	(-)	(X)	(-)	(-)	(X)
Swaziland	-4.4	-8.3	77	1.2	6.2	185	5.6	14.5	136	5.9	15.1	136
Sweden	-428.6	-1,158.3	24	416.1	1,053.8	49	844.6	2,212.1	36	866.3	2,277.6	36
Switzerland	120.0	-749.2	29	2,782.7	6,660.6	14	2,662.7	7,409.8	14	2,688.8	7,478.9	14
Syria	-0.3	-1.0	90	0.6	0.8	208	0.9	1.8	174	0.9	1.9	175
Taiwan	-949.5	-3,036.8	17	2,351.4	6,287.3	16	3,300.9	9,324.1	12	3,417.0	9,653.9	12
Tajikistan	-0.3	1.0	117	1.2	3.7	193	1.4	2.7	167	1.5	2.8	167
Tanzania	18.6	30.9	168	26.6	56.7	124	8.0	25.7	121	8.1	26.3	123
Thailand	-1,262.2	-3,252.9	16	1,042.0	2,984.2	25	2,304.2	6,237.1	20	2,379.8	6,439.8	20
Timor-Leste	0.0	0.1	100	0.0	0.1	224	0.0	0.0	222	0.0	0.0	222
Togo	80.0	205.7	205	81.0	209.2	86	0.9	3.5	164	1.0	3.7	164
Tokelau	0.0	-0.1	91	0.0	0.0	230	0.0	0.1	205	0.0	0.1	205
Tonga	1.2	3.4	131	1.3	3.8	191	0.1	0.4	193	0.2	0.5	192
Trinidad and Tobago	-308.7	-867.2	27	193.3	563.2	57	502.0	1,430.4	44	532.6	1,511.2	43
Tunisia	-28.1	18.5	156	31.6	217.9	82	59.8	199.4	80	62.4	206.1	80
Turkey	463.4	1,057.7	223	1,068.3	2,784.8	27	604.9	1,727.1	39	636.0	1,812.3	39
Turkmenistan	176.0	187.7	200	176.9	190.2	91	0.9	2.5	168	1.0	2.7	168
Turks and Caicos Islands	21.0	63.4	181	21.6	64.7	122	0.6	1.3	180	0.7	1.4	180
Tuvalu	0.1	0.2	103	0.1	0.2	223	0.0	0.0	223	0.0	0.0	223
Uganda	7.5	15.9	153	10.2	24.2	148	2.6	8.2	146	2.8	8.7	146
Ukraine	44.3	210.3	206	129.0	415.3	68	84.7	205.0	79	88.5	214.2	79
United Arab Emirates	1,569.1	4,683.6	232	1,786.2	5,311.9	17	217.1	628.3	62	226.7	655.3	62
United Kingdom	-182.5	-732.0	31	4,521.0	11,994.4	6	4,703.5	12,726.4	8	4,793.0	12,962.7	8
Uruguay	117.4	357.0	212	152.0	452.8	66	34.6	95.8	92	35.6	98.9	92
Uzbekistan	17.3	31.1	169	19.2	34.9	139	1.9	3.7	163	2.0	3.8	163
Vanuatu	-0.5	15.3	152	0.5	17.2	156	1.0	1.9	173	1.0	2.0	172
Vatican City	0.0	0.2	102	0.1	0.4	216	0.0	0.2	198	0.0	0.2	199
Venezuela	-1,821.3	-5,935.6	8	696.7	1,978.8	35	2,518.1	7,914.4	13	2,572.8	8,111.3	13
Vietnam	-1,587.7	-5,099.1	10	529.2	1,488.3	42	2,117.0	6,587.4	16	2,216.1	6,899.8	16
Wallis and Futuna	0.0	0.1	99	0.0	0.1	225	(-)	0.0	220	(-)	0.0	220
West Bank Administered by Israel	-0.2	-1.1	88	0.0	0.2	222	0.2	1.3	179	0.3	1.4	179
Western Sahara	(-)	0.0	95	(-)	(-)	(X)	(-)	0.0	221	(-)	0.0	221
Yemen	28.9	68.6	183	29.1	80.4	114	0.2	11.8	141	0.2	11.9	141
Zambia	8.3	29.5	167	14.3	40.3	135	6.0	10.9	142	6.0	10.9	143
Zimbabwe	0.6	6.3	138	4.9	14.8	161	4.3	8.5	145	4.3	8.9	145
Unidentified (1)	(-)	(-)	(X)	(-)	(-)	(X)	(-)	(-)	(X)	(-)	(-)	(X)

Exhibit 4a. Exports, Imports and Trade Balance by Country and Area, Not Seasonally Adjusted: 2014

In millions of dollars. Details may not equal totals due to rounding. (×) Not applicable. (-) Represents zero or less than one-half unit of measurement shown.

Country	Balance (Customs imports)			Exports Domestic & Foreign, F.A.S. basis			Imports Customs basis			Imports C.I.F. basis		
	March	Year-to-Date	Rank	March	Year-to-Date	Rank	March	Year-to-Date	Rank	March	Year-to-Date	Rank
Africa	-39.7	170.2	(X)	3,025.4	8,625.4	(X)	3,065.0	8,455.2	(X)	3,161.5	8,700.3	(X)
APEC	-36,718.9	-111,541.3	(X)	86,596.8	243,140.4	(X)	123,315.7	354,681.7	(X)	126,729.2	364,875.8	(X)
ASEAN	-4,025.8	-11,210.6	(X)	7,046.2	19,785.4	(X)	11,072.1	30,995.9	(X)	11,453.4	32,068.8	(X)
Asia - South	-2,736.6	-7,735.1	(X)	2,198.8	5,933.1	(X)	4,935.4	13,668.2	(X)	5,121.0	14,191.0	(X)
Asia Near East	-2,644.5	-11,483.6	(X)	6,443.2	16,831.5	(X)	9,087.7	28,315.1	(X)	9,338.2	29,066.6	(X)
CAFTA-DR	265.8	925.5	(X)	2,918.8	7,900.8	(X)	2,653.0	6,975.4	(X)	2,760.2	7,258.1	(X)
Central American Common Market	-55.6	39.0	(X)	2,211.9	6,009.2	(X)	2,267.5	5,970.2	(X)	2,363.0	6,224.8	(X)
Euro Area	-9,754.0	-24,360.5	(X)	18,414.7	50,874.6	(X)	28,168.7	75,235.1	(X)	28,811.7	76,837.3	(X)
Europe	-12,383.3	-31,611.5	(X)	30,644.1	82,979.0	(X)	43,027.4	114,590.5	(X)	44,039.1	117,129.1	(X)
European Union	-11,505.9	-29,396.6	(X)	24,565.8	67,022.8	(X)	36,071.7	96,419.4	(X)	36,886.6	98,480.9	(X)
LAFTA	-3,874.5	-10,166.6	(X)	30,345.2	87,091.9	(X)	34,219.6	97,258.4	(X)	34,816.1	99,105.8	(X)
NATO Allies	-10,459.8	-28,796.8	(X)	51,469.1	139,367.7	(X)	61,928.8	168,164.5	(X)	63,365.4	171,979.1	(X)
NICs	1,502.2	6,201.5	(X)	12,610.3	36,228.2	(X)	11,108.0	30,026.7	(X)	11,429.6	30,936.1	(X)
North America	-7,336.9	-20,260.7	(X)	47,044.6	130,452.8	(X)	54,381.4	150,713.5	(X)	55,265.5	153,260.0	(X)
OECD	-24,398.5	-65,973.8	(X)	88,194.5	242,611.7	(X)	112,593.0	308,585.4	(X)	114,864.6	314,793.9	(X)
OPEC	-5,192.5	-17,933.2	(X)	6,662.5	18,342.7	(X)	11,855.0	36,275.9	(X)	12,174.9	37,277.3	(X)
Pacific Rim Countries	-25,737.0	-81,719.6	(X)	34,801.5	98,919.6	(X)	60,538.6	180,639.2	(X)	62,684.0	187,214.7	(X)
South/Central America	3,316.9	7,347.9	(X)	16,042.2	44,695.7	(X)	12,725.3	37,347.7	(X)	13,229.6	38,860.6	(X)
Twenty Latin American Republics	-2,485.2	-6,490.0	(X)	34,479.3	98,012.7	(X)	36,964.5	104,502.7	(X)	37,671.0	106,639.6	(X)

Africa - Algeria, Angola, Benin, Botswana, British Indian Ocean Territories, Burkina Faso, Burundi, Cameroon, Cape Verde, Central African Republic, Chad, Comoros, Congo (Brazzaville), Congo (Kinshasa), Cote d'Ivoire, Djibouti, Egypt, Equatorial Guinea, Eritrea, Ethiopia, French Southern and Antarctic Lands, Gabon, Gambia, Ghana, Guinea, Guinea-Bissau, Kenya, Lesotho, Liberia, Libya, Madagascar, Malawi, Mali, Mauritania, Mauritius, Mayotte, Morocco, Mozambique, Namibia, Niger, Nigeria, Reunion, Rwanda, Sao Tome and Principe, Senegal, Seychelles, Sierra Leone, Somalia, South Africa, South Sudan, St. Helena, Sudan, Swaziland, Tanzania, Togo, Tunisia, Uganda, Western Sahara, Zambia, Zimbabwe.

APEC (Asia - Pacific Economic Cooperation) - Australia, Brunei, Canada, Chile, China, Hong Kong, Indonesia, Japan, Korea (South), Malaysia, Mexico, New Zealand, Papua New Guinea, Peru, Philippines, Russia, Singapore, Taiwan, Thailand, Vietnam.

ASEAN (Association of Southeast Asian Nations) - Brunei, Burma, Cambodia, Indonesia, Laos, Malaysia, Philippines, Singapore, Thailand, Vietnam.

Asia - South - Afghanistan, Bangladesh, India, Nepal, Pakistan, Sri Lanka.

Asia Near East - Bahrain, Gaza Strip Administered by Israel, Iran, Iraq, Israel, Jordan, Kuwait, Lebanon, Oman, Qatar, Saudi Arabia, Syria, United Arab Emirates, West Bank Administered by Israel, Yemen.

CAFTA-DR (Dominican Republic-Central America-United States Free Trade Agreement) - Costa Rica, Dominican Republic, El Salvador, Guatemala, Honduras, Nicaragua.

Central American Common Market - Costa Rica, El Salvador, Guatemala, Honduras, Nicaragua.

Euro Area - Austria, Belgium, Cyprus, Estonia, Finland, France, Germany, Greece Ireland, Italy, Latvia, Luxembourg, Malta, Netherlands, Portugal, Slovakia, Slovenia, Spain.

Europe - Albania, Andorra, Armenia, Austria, Azerbaijan, Belarus, Belgium, Bosnia-Herzegovina, Bulgaria, Croatia, Cyprus, Czech Republic, Denmark, Estonia, Faroe Islands, Finland, France, Georgia, Germany, Gibraltar, Greece, Hungary, Iceland, Ireland, Italy, Kazakhstan, Kosovo, Kyrgyzstan, Latvia, Liechtenstein, Lithuania, Luxembourg, Macedonia, Malta, Moldova, Monaco, Montenegro, Netherlands, Norway, Poland, Portugal, Romania, Russia, San Marino, Serbia, Slovakia, Slovenia, Spain, Svalbard, Jan Mayen Island, Sweden, Switzerland, Tajikistan, Turkey Turkmenistan, Ukraine, United Kingdom, Uzbekistan, Vatican City.

European Union - Austria, Belgium, Bulgaria, Croatia, Cyprus, Czech Republic, Denmark, Estonia, Finland, France, Germany, Greece, Hungary, Ireland, Italy, Latvia, Lithuania, Luxembourg, Malta, Netherlands, Poland, Portugal, Romania, Slovakia, Slovenia, Spain, Sweden, United Kingdom.

LAFTA (Latin American Free Trade Area) - Argentina, Bolivia, Brazil, Chile, Colombia, Ecuador, Mexico, Paraguay, Peru, Uruguay, Venezuela.

NATO (North Atlantic Treaty Organization) Allies - Belgium, Bulgaria, Canada, Czech Republic, Denmark, Estonia, France, Germany, Greece, Hungary, Iceland, Italy, Latvia, Lithuania, Luxembourg, Netherlands, Norway, Poland, Portugal, Romania, Slovakia, Slovenia, Spain, Turkey, United Kingdom.

NICs (Newly Industrialized Countries) - Hong Kong, Korea (South), Singapore, Taiwan.

North America - Canada, Mexico.

OECD (Organization for Economic Cooperation and Development) - Australia, Austria, Belgium, Canada, Chile, Czech Republic, Denmark, Estonia, Finland, France, Germany, Greece, Hungary, Iceland, Ireland, Israel, Italy, Japan, Korea (South), Luxembourg Mexico, Netherlands, New Zealand, Norway, Poland, Portugal, Slovakia, Slovenia, Spain, Sweden, Switzerland, Turkey, United Kingdom.

OPEC (Organization of the Petroleum Exporting Countries) - Algeria, Angola, Ecuador, Iran, Iraq, Kuwait, Libya, Nigeria, Qatar, Saudi Arabia, United Arab Emirates, Venezuela.

Pacific Rim Countries - Australia, Brunei, China, Hong Kong, Indonesia, Japan, Korea (South), Macau, Malaysia, New Zealand, Papua New Guinea, Philippines, Singapore, Taiwan.

South/Central America - Anguilla, Antigua and Barbuda, Argentina, Aruba, Bahamas, Barbados, Belize, Bermuda, Bolivia, Brazil, British Virgin Islands, Cayman Islands, Chile, Colombia, Costa Rica, Cuba, Curacao, Dominica, Dominican Republic, Ecuador, El Salvador, Falkland Islands (Islas Malvinas), French Guiana, Grenada, Guadeloupe, Guatemala, Guyana, Haiti, Honduras, Jamaica, Martinique, Montserrat, Nicaragua, Panama, Paraguay, Peru, St. Kitts and Nevis, Sint Maarten, St. Lucia, St. Vincent and the Grenadines, Suriname, Trinidad and Tobago, Turks and Caicos Islands, Uruguay, Venezuela.

Twenty Latin American Republics - Argentina, Bolivia, Brazil, Chile, Colombia, Costa Rica, Cuba, Dominican Republic, Ecuador, El Salvador, Guatemala, Haiti, Honduras, Mexico, Nicaragua, Panama, Paraguay, Peru, Uruguay, Venezuela.

(1) The export totals reflect shipments of certain grains, oilseeds, and satellites that are not included in the country/area totals.

NOTE: Area data reflect the composition of the areas at yearend. ☐